OPPOSING VIEWPOINTS® SERIES

Voting Rights

Other Books of Related Interest

Opposing Viewpoints Series

The Democratic Party

Illegal Immigration

The Republican Party

US Foreign Policy

At Issue Series

The Affordable Care Act

Minorities and the Law

Negative Campaigning

The Wealth Divide

Current Controversies Series

Immigration

Politics and Religion

Racial Profiling

The Wage Gap

"Congress shall make no law . . . abridging the freedom of speech, or of the press."

First Amendment to the US Constitution

The basic foundation of our democracy is the First Amendment guarantee of freedom of expression. The Opposing Viewpoints series is dedicated to the concept of this basic freedom and the idea that it is more important to practice it than to enshrine it.

OPPOSING VIEWPOINTS® SERIES

Voting Rights

Noah Berlatsky, Book Editor

GREENHAVEN PRESS
A part of Gale, Cengage Learning

GALE
CENGAGE Learning·

Farmington Hills, Mich • San Francisco • New York • Waterville, Maine
Meriden, Conn • Mason, Ohio • Chicago

Patricia Coryell, *Vice President & Publisher, New Products & GVRL*
Douglas Dentino, *Manager, New Products*
Judy Galens, *Acquisitions Editor*

LIBRARY OF CONGRESS CATALOGING-IN-PUBLICATION DATA

Voting rights / Noah Berlatsky, book editor.
    pages cm. -- -- (Opposing viewpoints) "Opposing Viewpoints is the leading source for libraries and classrooms in need of current-issue materials. The viewpoints are selected from a wide range of highly respected sources and publications"-- Provided by publisher.
    Includes bibliographical references and index.
    ISBN 978-0-7377-7300-2 (hardback) -- ISBN 978-0-7377-7301-9 (paperback)
    1. Suffrage--United States--History--Juvenile literature. 2. Voting--United States--History--Juvenile literature. 3. Minorities--Suffrage--United States--History. 4. United States. Voting Rights Act of 1965--Juvenile literature. 5. United States--Politics and government--Juvenile literature. I. Berlatsky, Noah.
    JK1846.V7 2015
    324.6'20973--dc23
                                                              2014030223

Printed in the United States of America
1 2 3 4 5   19 18 17 16 15

Contents

Chapter 3: How Do Voting Rights Apply to Particular Groups?

Why Consider Opposing Viewpoints?

> "The only way in which a human being can make some approach to knowing the whole of a subject is by hearing what can be said about it by persons of every variety of opinion and studying all modes in which it can be looked at by every character of mind. No wise man ever acquired his wisdom in any mode but this."
>
> John Stuart Mill

In our media-intensive culture it is not difficult to find differing opinions. Thousands of newspapers and magazines and dozens of radio and television talk shows resound with differing points of view. The difficulty lies in deciding which opinion to agree with and which "experts" seem the most credible. The more inundated we become with differing opinions and claims, the more essential it is to hone critical reading and thinking skills to evaluate these ideas. Opposing Viewpoints books address this problem directly by presenting stimulating debates that can be used to enhance and teach these skills. The varied opinions contained in each book examine many different aspects of a single issue. While examining these conveniently edited opposing views, readers can develop critical thinking skills such as the ability to compare and contrast authors' credibility, facts, argumentation styles, use of persuasive techniques, and other stylistic tools. In short, the Opposing Viewpoints Series is an ideal way to attain the higher-level thinking and reading skills so essential in a culture of diverse and contradictory opinions.

In addition to providing a tool for critical thinking, Opposing Viewpoints books challenge readers to question their own strongly held opinions and assumptions. Most people form their opinions on the basis of upbringing, peer pressure, and personal, cultural, or professional bias. By reading carefully balanced opposing views, readers must directly confront new ideas as well as the opinions of those with whom they disagree. This is not to argue simplistically that everyone who reads opposing views will—or should—change his or her opinion. Instead, the series enhances readers' understanding of their own views by encouraging confrontation with opposing ideas. Careful examination of others' views can lead to the readers' understanding of the logical inconsistencies in their own opinions, perspective on why they hold an opinion, and the consideration of the possibility that their opinion requires further evaluation.

Evaluating Other Opinions

To ensure that this type of examination occurs, Opposing Viewpoints books present all types of opinions. Prominent spokespeople on different sides of each issue as well as well-known professionals from many disciplines challenge the reader. An additional goal of the series is to provide a forum for other, less known, or even unpopular viewpoints. The opinion of an ordinary person who has had to make the decision to cut off life support from a terminally ill relative, for example, may be just as valuable and provide just as much insight as a medical ethicist's professional opinion. The editors have two additional purposes in including these less known views. One, the editors encourage readers to respect others' opinions—even when not enhanced by professional credibility. It is only by reading or listening to and objectively evaluating others' ideas that one can determine whether they are worthy of consideration. Two, the inclusion of such viewpoints encourages the important critical thinking skill of objectively evaluating an author's credentials and bias. This evaluation will illuminate an author's reasons for taking a particular stance on an issue and will aid in readers' evaluation of the author's ideas.

It is our hope that these books will give readers a deeper understanding of the issues debated and an appreciation of the complexity of even seemingly simple issues when good and honest people disagree. This awareness is particularly important in a democratic society such as ours in which people enter into public debate to determine the common good. Those with whom one disagrees should not be regarded as enemies but rather as people whose views deserve careful examination and may shed light on one's own.

Thomas Jefferson once said that "difference of opinion leads to inquiry, and inquiry to truth." Jefferson, a broadly educated man, argued that "if a nation expects to be ignorant and free ... it expects what never was and never will be." As individuals and as a nation, it is imperative that we consider the opinions of others and examine them with skill and discernment. The Opposing Viewpoints series is intended to help readers achieve this goal.

David L. Bender and Bruno Leone,
Founders

Introduction

> *"Throughout the Florida electoral stale-*
> *mate, a variety of courts were asked to*
> *intervene selectively to try to address a*
> *parade of competing electoral horrors.*
> *Congress cannot shy away from its own*
> *obligation to ensure that no presidential*
> *election is ever decided in such a man-*
> *ner again."*
>
> —New York Times,
> *"The Ballot Reform Imperative",*
> *December 17, 2000*

In the 2000 presidential election, voters did not choose the president; instead, the Supreme Court did. In the election, Democratic candidate Al Gore won the popular vote nation-wide. However, presidential elections are decided by statewide electoral votes—and there Gore was virtually tied with Repub-lican candidate George W. Bush. Whichever candidate won Florida would win the election.

Initially, Bush led by about eighteen hundred votes, trig-gering an automatic machine recount. Once that was done, Bush's lead was cut to only 327 votes out of six million total. The Florida Supreme Court ordered a manual recount in cer-tain counties. However, the Supreme Court of the United States, in *Bush v. Gore*, overturned that ruling, and in a vote split along partisan lines, the conservative majority declared that the manual recount was invalid. Bush became president—even though later studies showed that Gore actually received more votes and would have won if a manual recount of the state had been held, as reported by Martin Kettle in a January 28, 2001, article at the *Guardian*.

There have been many critics of the *Bush v. Gore* decision. Some are concerned that it not only undermined the voting rights of those who voted in 2000 but also may have damaged the voting rights of Americans in the long term. The decision itself explicitly declares that US citizens are not guaranteed a vote in presidential elections:

> The individual citizen has no federal constitutional right to vote for electors for the President of the United States unless and until the state legislature chooses a statewide election as the means to implement its power to appoint members of the Electoral College.

Jo McKeegan, writing in a December 14, 2010, post at Fair Vote.org, concluded that "a state could completely deny its citizens a chance to vote in presidential races" and added that this "underscores the range of other ways our right to vote can be diluted and weakened by federal, state, and local laws without recourse." McKeegan points out that while there were some technical changes to voting machines, the 2000 election did not prompt a reevaluation of local election laws. States still decide their own recount laws, without federal guidelines. "In nearly all states," McKeegan concludes, "a timely recount in a presidential election remains impossible to conduct today." The 2000 election debacle could happen again, and Americans could once more be denied their choice of president.

There have been some arguably positive results for voting rights from the *Bush v. Gore* decision, however. The majority opinion in the case invalidated the Florida state recount efforts on the grounds that they were not consistent and tended to "value one person's vote over those of another." This seems to give some precedent for the idea that voters have a right to have their votes valued equally and that there is a constitutional guarantee of equal voting rights.

Whether *Bush v. Gore* will provide a basis for broad equal protection in voting seems unclear. The Supreme Court itself has cited the case as a precedent only once, in a dissent by Justice Clarence Thomas written thirteen years after the original ruling. In fact, in the *Bush v. Gore* decision itself, the justices declared, "Our consideration is limited to the present circumstances, for the problem of equal protection in election processes generally presents many complexities"—virtually insisting that the decision not be used as a precedent in other cases.

Despite the Supreme Court's own reticence, other courts have begun to use the equal protection principles in their decisions. This is especially the case in some 2012 federal court decisions involving Ohio, according to Richard L. Hasen in an October 26, 2012, article in *Slate*. Hasen points out that a federal judge forced Ohio to restore the final weekend of early voting before the 2012 election based on the equal protection standard in *Bush v. Gore*. "The judge," according to Hasen, "suggested that once Ohio had added the early voting days, it couldn't take them away, or at least couldn't take them away from everyone except military voters." Another case in Ohio held that provisional ballots that were cast in the wrong polling place because of errors on the part of poll workers still had to be counted in the election results. Perhaps in the future, then, *Bush v. Gore*, which took an election out of the hands of voters, may end up strengthening Americans' voting rights.

The remainder of this book looks at other controversies surrounding voting rights in chapters titled "Are Voting Rights Act Protections Still Necessary?," "Are States Restricting Voting Rights?," "How Do Voting Rights Apply to Particular Groups?," and "Can Changing Voting Procedures Promote Fairness and Equality?" These issues call into question what constitutional rights Americans have to vote and how states can, or should, provide access to the ballot.

OPPOSING
VIEWPOINTS®
SERIES

CHAPTER 1

Are Voting Rights Act Protections Still Necessary?

Chapter Preface

In June 2013, the Supreme Court struck down key provisions of the Voting Rights Act (VRA). The act, passed in 1965, allowed the federal government to veto and roll back discriminatory voting regulations in southern states that prevented African Americans from voting. Sections 4 and 5 of the act gave the federal government the ability to reject new voting laws in certain states, mostly in the South, if the laws were discriminatory. In its 2013 decision, however, the Supreme Court decided that voting discrimination was no longer a serious problem in the South and that it was unconstitutional for the federal government to continue to interfere in state election laws.

Many people believed that the invalidation of Sections 4 and 5 would effectively gut the Voting Rights Act, making it useless. However, that is not exactly what has happened. Instead, with Sections 4 and 5 invalidated, Section 2 of the act has taken on new importance. According to Nicholas Stephanopoulos in an October 23, 2013, article at *Slate*,

> Section 2 is the VRA's core remaining prohibition of racial discrimination in voting. It bans practices that make it more difficult for minority voters to "participate in the political process" and "elect representatives of their choice." It applies to both redistricting (as in Texas) and voting restrictions (as in North Carolina).

Stephanopoulos goes on to argue that Section 2 is relatively ineffective at preventing redistricting, which can split minority voters into a number of districts and thus dilute their electoral power. However, Section 2 has been somewhat effective in preventing voting restrictions such as tight voter registration rules or polling place reductions. Stephanopoulos said that challenges to such restrictions under Section 2 have been upheld in eighteen cases since 1982, which is a success rate of about 50 percent. Under Section 5, restrictions could be vetoed by the federal government before they were put into place; Section 2 cannot do that, but some protections still remain.

Stephanopoulos's arguments seem to be borne out by recent voting rights cases. In Wisconsin in early 2014, a federal judge invalidated a restrictive voter identification (ID) law under Section 2. A lawsuit in Ohio against that state's restrictions on early voting, which the suit says will disproportionately affect minority voters, is also being made on Section 2 grounds. Ohio State University election law professor Daniel Tokaji said, "I think it's exactly what the federal courts should be doing. . . . When partisan politicians go too far to restrict the right to vote in an effort to serve their own ends, courts aren't likely to look on that kindly," as quoted by Zachary Roth in a May 6, 2014, post on the MSNBC website.

Not all commenters are pleased with this use of Section 2, however. Heritage Foundation fellow Hans A. von Spakovsky argues in a May 2, 2014, article at *National Review Online* that using Section 2 to strike down voter ID laws is unnecessary and unconstitutional. Von Spakovsky says there is no evidence that voter ID laws have damaged minority voters in the past and also takes exception to the judge's ruling that Wisconsin's voter ID law would hurt low-income voters. "Not only is that factually unsupportable," von Spakovsky says, "but 'low-income voters' are not even a protected class under Section 2 of the Voting Rights Act, which prohibits racial discrimination in voting."

The authors of the viewpoints in the following chapter examine other controversies surrounding the Voting Rights Act and debate whether the act's protections are still necessary.

> "Section 4 of the Voting Rights Act is unconstitutional; its formula can no longer be used as a basis for subjecting jurisdictions to preclearance."

The Court Was Right to Strike Down Section 4 of the Voting Rights Act

John Roberts

John Roberts is the chief justice of the United States Supreme Court. In the following viewpoint, he argues that Section 4 of the Voting Rights Act of 1965 is unconstitutional. The section originally put limitations on certain states so that they could not pass voting laws without federal clearance. The rationale for this, Roberts says, was that when the law was passed the states in question had recently put in place laws restricting voting in racist ways and that the states had very low voter turnout. Roberts says this was true in the 1960s. However, he says, times have changed, and the racist voting laws in question have long been repealed. Therefore, he concludes, since abuses are long past, there are no longer grounds to abridge the authority of the states.

John Roberts, *Shelby County v. Holder*, US Supreme Court, June 25, 2013.

As you read, consider the following questions:

1. When were the coverage formula and preclearance requirement of Section 4 initially supposed to expire?

2. What does the Tenth Amendment to the Constitution say, and why does Roberts say it is relevant to this case?

3. Which justices agreed with Roberts in this case, and which disagreed with him?

The Voting Rights Act of 1965 was enacted to address entrenched racial discrimination in voting, "an insidious and pervasive evil which had been perpetuated in certain parts of our country through unremitting and ingenious defiance of the Constitution." *South Carolina v. Katzenbach*, 383 U.S. 301, 309. Section 2 of the act, which bans any "standard, practice, or procedure" that "results in a denial or abridgement of the right of any citizen ... to vote on account of race or color," 42 U.S.C. § 1973(a), applies nationwide, is permanent, and is not at issue in this case. Other sections apply only to some parts of the country. Section 4 of the act provides the "coverage formula," defining the "covered jurisdictions" as states or political subdivisions that maintained tests or devices as prerequisites to voting, and had low voter registration or turnout, in the 1960s and early 1970s. §1973b(b). In those covered jurisdictions, §5 of the act provides that no change in voting procedures can take effect until approved by specified federal authorities in Washington, D.C. §1973c(a). Such approval is known as "preclearance."

Section 4 Unconstitutional

The coverage formula and preclearance requirement were initially set to expire after five years, but the act has been reauthorized several times. In 2006, the act was reauthorized for an additional 25 years, but the coverage formula was not changed. Coverage still turned on whether a jurisdiction had a voting test in the 1960s or 1970s, and had low voter registration or turnout at that time. Shortly after the 2006 reauthorization, a Texas utility district sought to bail out from the act's coverage and, in the alternative, challenged the act's constitutionality. This court resolved the challenge on statutory grounds, but expressed serious doubts about the act's continued constitutionality. See *Northwest Austin Municipal Util. Dist. No. One v. Holder*, 557 U.S. 193.

Petitioner Shelby County, in the covered jurisdiction of Alabama, sued the attorney general in federal district court in Washington, D.C., seeking a declaratory judgment that Sections 4(b) and 5 are facially unconstitutional, as well as a permanent injunction against their enforcement. The district court upheld the act, finding that the evidence before Congress in 2006 was sufficient to justify reauthorizing §5 and continuing §4(b)'s coverage formula. The D.C. circuit affirmed. After surveying the evidence in the record, that court accepted Congress's conclusion that §2 litigation remained inadequate in the covered jurisdictions to protect the rights of minority voters, that §5 was therefore still necessary, and that the coverage formula continued to pass constitutional muster.

Held: Section 4 of the Voting Rights Act is unconstitutional; its formula can no longer be used as a basis for subjecting jurisdictions to preclearance.

(a) In *Northwest Austin*, this court noted that the Voting Rights Act "imposes current burdens and must be justified by current needs" and concluded that "a departure from the fundamental principle of equal sovereignty requires a showing that a statute's disparate geographic coverage is sufficiently related to the problem that it targets." 557 U.S., at 203. These basic principles guide review of the question presented here.

(1) State legislation may not contravene federal law. States retain broad autonomy, however, in structuring their governments and pursuing legislative objectives. Indeed, the Tenth Amendment reserves to the states all powers not specifically

granted to the federal government, including "the power to regulate elections." *Gregory v. Ashcroft*, 501 U.S. 452, 461–462. There is also a "fundamental principle of equal sovereignty" among the states, which is highly pertinent in assessing disparate treatment of states. *Northwest Austin, supra*, at 203.

The Voting Rights Act sharply departs from these basic principles. It requires states to beseech the federal government for permission to implement laws that they would otherwise have the right to enact and execute on their own. And despite the tradition of equal sovereignty, the act applies to only nine states (and additional counties). That is why, in 1966, this court described the act as "stringent" and "potent," *Katzenbach*, 383 U.S., at 308, 315, 337. The court nonetheless upheld the act, concluding that such an "uncommon exercise of congressional power" could be justified by "exceptional conditions." *Id.*, at 334.

(2) In 1966, these departures were justified by the "blight of racial discrimination in voting" that had "infected the electoral process in parts of our country for nearly a century," *Katzenbach*, 383 U.S., at 308. At the time, the coverage formula—the means of linking the exercise of the unprecedented authority with the problem that warranted it—made sense. The act was limited to areas where Congress found "evidence of actual voting discrimination," and the covered jurisdictions shared two characteristics: "the use of tests and devices for voter registration, and a voting rate in the 1964 presidential election at least 12 points below the national average." *Id.*, at 330. The court explained that "[t]ests and devices are relevant to voting discrimination because of their long history as a tool for perpetrating the evil; a low voting rate is pertinent for the obvious reason that widespread disenfranchisement must inevitably affect the number of actual voters." *Ibid.* The court therefore concluded that "the coverage formula [was] rational in both practice and theory."

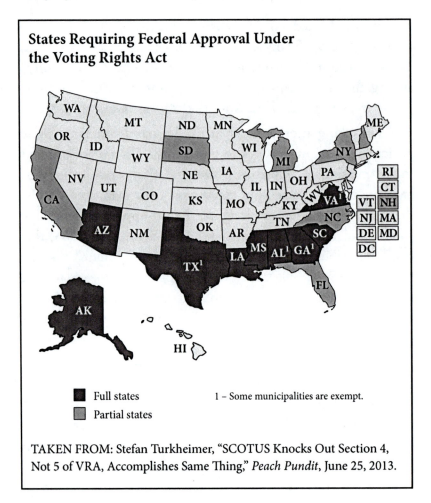

States Requiring Federal Approval Under the Voting Rights Act

Full states

Partial states

1 – Some municipalities are exempt.

TAKEN FROM: Stefan Turkheimer, "SCOTUS Knocks Out Section 4, Not 5 of VRA, Accomplishes Same Thing," *Peach Pundit*, June 25, 2013.

Dramatic Change

(3) Nearly 50 years later, things have changed dramatically. Largely because of the Voting Rights Act, "[v]oter turnout and registration rates" in covered jurisdictions "now approach parity. Blatantly discriminatory evasions of federal decrees are rare. And minority candidates hold office at unprecedented levels." *Northwest Austin, supra,* at 202. The tests and devices that blocked ballot access have been forbidden nationwide for over 40 years. Yet the act has not eased §5's restrictions or narrowed the scope of §4's coverage formula along the way.

Instead those extraordinary and unprecedented features have been reauthorized as if nothing has changed, and they have grown even stronger. Because §5 applies only to those jurisdictions singled out by §4, the court turns to consider that provision.

(b) Section 4's formula is unconstitutional in light of current conditions.

(1) In 1966, the coverage formula was "rational in both practice and theory." *Katzenbach, supra,* at 330. It looked to cause (discriminatory tests) and effect (low voter registration and turnout), and tailored the remedy (preclearance) to those jurisdictions exhibiting both. By 2009, however, the "coverage formula raise[d] serious constitutional questions." *Northwest Austin, supra,* at 204. Coverage today is based on decades-old data and eradicated practices. The formula captures states by reference to literacy tests and low voter registration and turnout in the 1960s and early 1970s. But such tests have been banned for over 40 years. And voter registration and turnout numbers in covered states have risen dramatically. In 1965, the states could be divided into those with a recent history of voting tests and low voter registration and turnout and those without those characteristics. Congress based its coverage formula on that distinction. Today the nation is no longer divided along those lines, yet the Voting Rights Act continues to treat it as if it were.

History Did Not End

(2) The government attempts to defend the formula on grounds that it is "reverse-engineered"—Congress identified the jurisdictions to be covered and *then* came up with criteria to describe them. *Katzenbach* did not sanction such an approach, reasoning instead that the coverage formula was rational because the "formula . . . was relevant to the problem." 383 U.S., at 329, 330. The government has a fallback argument— because the formula was relevant in 1965, its continued use is

permissible so long as any discrimination remains in the states identified in 1965. But this does not look to "current political conditions," *Northwest Austin, supra,* at 203, instead relying on a comparison between the states in 1965. But history did not end in 1965. In assessing the "current need[]" for a preclearance system treating states differently from one another today, history since 1965 cannot be ignored. The Fifteenth Amendment is not designed to punish for the past; its purpose is to ensure a better future. To serve that purpose, Congress—if it is to divide the states—must identify those jurisdictions to be singled out on a basis that makes sense in light of current conditions.

(3) Respondents also rely heavily on data from the record compiled by Congress before reauthorizing the act. Regardless of how one looks at that record, no one can fairly say that it shows anything approaching the "pervasive," "flagrant," "widespread," and "rampant" discrimination that clearly distinguished the covered jurisdictions from the rest of the nation in 1965. *Katzenbach, supra,* at 308, 315, 331. But a more fundamental problem remains: Congress did not use that record to fashion a coverage formula grounded in current conditions. It instead re-enacted a formula based on 40-year-old facts having no logical relation to the present day.

Roberts, C.J. [chief], delivered the opinion of the court, in which [Antonin] Scalia, [Anthony] Kennedy, [Clarence] Thomas, and [Samuel] Alito, JJ. [justices], joined. Thomas, J., filed a concurring opinion. [Ruth Bader] Ginsburg, J., filed a dissenting opinion, in which [Stephen] Breyer, [Sonia] Sotomayor, and [Elena] Kagan, JJ., joined.

"State election laws that were enacted after 1877 were disastrous for black citizens."

The Court Should Not Have Struck Down Section 4 of the Voting Rights Act

John Paul Stevens

John Paul Stevens is a former justice of the United States Supreme Court. In the following viewpoint, he argues that the Supreme Court was wrong to invalidate the provisions of the Voting Rights Act that place restrictions on certain states' voting rights laws. He argues that there has been an extensive history of discrimination in the United States against blacks, especially against their voting rights. Congress decided that the Voting Rights Act was required to remedy that. Stevens argues that the Supreme Court should honor that decision rather than overturn a decision made by the people's representatives.

As you read, consider the following questions:

1. What specific effects did the passage of state election laws in 1877 have on black citizens in the South, according to Stevens?

2. How did Article I, Section 2 of the Constitution create a serious inequality among the states, in Stevens's opinion?

3. What happened at the Edmund Pettus Bridge in 1965?

In *Bending Toward Justice*, Professor Gary May describes a number of the conflicts between white supremacists in Alabama and nonviolent civil rights workers that led to the enactment of the Voting Rights Act of 1965—often just called the VRA. The book also describes political developments that influenced President Lyndon Johnson to support the act in 1965, and later events that supported the congressional reenactments of the VRA signed by President Richard Nixon in 1970, by President Gerald Ford in 1975, by President Ronald Reagan in 1982, and by President George W. Bush in 2006.

Shelby County v. Holder

May's eminently readable book is particularly timely because the Supreme Court, on June 25, 2013, issued its decision in *Shelby County v. Holder*, invalidating the portion of the 2006 enactment that retained the formula used in the 1965 act to determine which states and political subdivisions must obtain the approval of the Department of Justice, or the US District Court in the District of Columbia, before changes in their election laws may become effective. That formula imposed a "preclearance" requirement on states that had maintained a "test or device" as a prerequisite to voting on November 1, 1964, and had less than a 50 percent voter registration or turnout in the 1964 presidential election. Alabama, where Shelby County is located, is one of those states. Over the dissent of Alabama-born Justice Hugo Black, the court had upheld the preclearance provision shortly after the VRA was enacted in 1966 in *South Carolina v. Katzenbach*.

May's book contains a wealth of information about the events that led to the enactment of the 1965 statute—and about the dedication and heroism of little-known participants in the events that came to national attention in 1964 and 1965. It includes both favorable and unfavorable information about well-known figures like Martin Luther King Jr. and J. Edgar Hoover, and about some of the methods used by whites to prevent blacks from voting and from registering to vote.

In his prologue, the author makes it clear that in the 1960s in the Deep South not only were African Americans prohibited from voting, but it was dangerous for them to attempt to do so. He describes the contrast between the oppression during the 1960s and the conditions a century earlier during the period that later became known as "Radical Reconstruction." During the decade after the Civil War, when the South was divided into military districts occupied by federal troops, southern blacks enthusiastically embraced their newly acquired political freedom:

> As many as two thousand served as state legislators, city councilmen, tax assessors, justices of the peace, jurors, sheriffs, and US marshals; fourteen black politicians entered the House of Representatives; and two became US senators.

Although he does not identify the withdrawal of federal troops in 1876 as the principal cause of the change, May notes that by 1877 "southern white Democrats had overthrown every new state government and established state constitutions that stripped black citizens of their political rights." Terrorist groups "like the Ku Klux Klan and the Knights of the White Camellia destroyed black schools and churches and murdered at will."

State election laws that were enacted after 1877 were disastrous for black citizens. Whereas 130,000 blacks had been registered to vote in Louisiana in 1896, only 1,342 were registered to vote in 1904. In Alabama only 2 percent of eligible black adults were registered, and they risked serious reprisals it they attempted to exercise their right to vote. Black disenfranchisement, like segregation, was nearly complete throughout the

South for well over sixty years. It was enforced not only by discriminatory laws, but also by official and unofficial uses of violence.

Have Things Changed?

Writing for the five-man majority in *Shelby County*, the recently decided Supreme Court case challenging the VRA, Chief Justice John Roberts noted that "times have changed" since 1965. The tests and devices that blocked African American access to the ballot in 1965 have been forbidden nationwide for over forty-eight years; the levels of registration and voting by African Americans in southern states are now comparable to, or greater than, those of whites.

Moreover, the two southern cities, Philadelphia, Mississippi and Selma, Alabama, where the most publicized misconduct by white police officials occurred in 1964 and 1965, now have African American mayors. In view of the changes that have occurred in the South, the majority concluded that the current enforcement of the preclearance requirement against the few states identified in the statute violates an unwritten rule requiring Congress to treat all of the states as equal sovereigns.

The court's heavy reliance on the importance of a "fundamental principle of *equal* sovereignty among the states," while supported by language in an earlier opinion by Chief Justice Roberts, ignored the fact that Article I, Section 2 of the Constitution created a serious inequality among the states. That clause counted "three fifths" of a state's slaves for the purpose of measuring the size of its congressional delegation and its representation in the Electoral College. That provision was offensive because it treated African Americans as though each of them was equal to only three-fifths of a white person, but it was even more offensive because it increased the power of the southern states by counting three-fifths of their slaves even though those slaves were not allowed to vote. The northern states would have been politically better off if the slave population had been simply omitted from the number used to measure the voting power of the slave states.

The fact that this "slave bonus" created a basic inequality between the slave states and the free states has often been overlooked, as has its far-reaching impact. In 1800, for example, that bonus determined the outcome of the presidential election since it then gave the southern states an extra nine or ten votes in the Electoral College, and Thomas Jefferson prevailed over John Adams by only eight electoral votes. Because of the slave bonus, Adams served only one term as president.

The slave bonus unfairly enhanced the power of the southern states in Congress throughout the period prior to the Civil War. It was after the war that Section 2 of the Fourteenth Amendment, passed in 1868, put an end to the slave bonus. When the Fifteenth Amendment was ratified in 1870 during the [Ulysses S.] Grant administration, the size of the southern states' congressional delegations was governed by the number of citizens eligible to vote. Since that number included blacks as well as whites, during Reconstruction those states were no longer overrepresented in either Congress or the Electoral College.

After Reconstruction ended, however, the terrorist tactics of the Ku Klux Klan and other groups devoted to the cause of white supremacy effectively prevented any significant voting at all by African Americans, thus replacing a prewar three-fifths bonus with a post-Reconstruction bonus of 100 percent of the nonvoting African Americans. Thus, for almost a century—until the VRA was enacted during President Johnson's administration—the southern states' representation in Congress was significantly larger than it should have been.

History Did Not Begin in 1890

Both the underrepresentation of blacks and the overrepresentation of white supremacists in the South during that period contradict the notion that the "fundamental principle of equal sovereignty among the states" is a part of our unwritten Constitution. As Justice [Ruth Bader] Ginsburg pointed out in her largely unanswered dissent in the *Shelby County* case, the court in its opinion upholding the original 1965 Voting Rights Act

> held, in no uncertain terms, that the principle [of equal sovereignty] "*applies only to the terms upon which States are admitted to the Union,* and not to the remedies for local evils which have subsequently appeared."

Except for his reference to the fact that the first century of congressional enforcement of the Fifteenth Amendment's guarantee of the right to vote "can only be regarded as a failure," Chief Justice Roberts's opinion gives the reader the impression that the Voting Rights Act was Congress's response to a specific problem that developed in the 1890s. Parroting Chief Justice Earl Warren's opinion in *South Carolina v. Katzenbach* Chief Justice Roberts wrote:

> In the 1890s, Alabama, Georgia, Louisiana, Mississippi, North Carolina, South Carolina, and Virginia began to enact literacy tests for voter registration and to employ other methods designed to prevent African Americans from voting.

There is no reference in the opinion to anything that happened before 1890. By selecting two examples—Philadelphia, Mississippi, and Selma, Alabama, where black mayors now preside—to illustrate the magnitude of the change that has taken place since 1965, however, Roberts ironically emphasizes the fact that the "tests or devices" that were used in the statute's coverage formula were not the principal means by which white supremacists prevented blacks from voting.

The contrast between Roberts's recent opinion and Justice Abe Fortas's opinion in *United States v. Price* (1966), the case arising out of the Mississippi incident, is striking. While the chief justice's opinion notes that "three men were murdered while working in the area to register African-American voters," Justice Fortas explained that the murders occurred after the three men had been taken into custody and police officers had taken them to a rendezvous with fifteen conspirators to "punish" them. In discussing the statutory issues presented by the case, Justice Fortas noted that the

> purpose and scope of the 1866 and 1870 enactments must be viewed against the events and passions of the time. The Civil War had ended in April 1865. Relations between Negroes and whites were increasingly turbulent. Congress had taken control of the entire governmental process in former Confederate States. . . . For a few years "radical" Republicans dominated the governments of the southern states and Negroes played a substantial political role. But countermeasures were swift and violent. The Ku Klux Klan was organized by southern whites in 1866 and a similar organization appeared with the romantic title of the Knights of the White Camellia. In 1868 a wave of murders and assaults was launched including assassinations designed to keep Negroes from the polls.

Nothing that happened before the 1890s is even mentioned in Roberts's opinion for the court in the *Shelby County* case.

Bloody Sunday

The story of "Bloody Sunday" in Selma, Alabama, where, as the chief justice notes, "police beat and used tear gas against hundreds marching in support of African American enfranchisement," is told in detail in May's book. Given the fact that 57 percent of the residents of Selma are black, it is not at all surprising that the city now has a black mayor. What is remarkable is the fact that so few members of that majority were registered to vote in 1965.

May's description of the conditions in Selma begins with an account of the work of Bernard Lafayette, who, as a twenty-one-year-old member of the Student Nonviolent Coordinating Committee, moved into the city in 1962 to encourage blacks to register to vote. Lafayette's commitment to nonviolent resistance to segregation, which had its origins in his religious training, was confirmed during the student sit-ins in Nashville in 1960.

Lafayette's experiences in Selma during 1962 illuminate some of the ways in which the white minority prevented blacks from voting—by simple stonewalling in response to repeated attempts to register; by requiring them to pass impossibly difficult tests to qualify to vote; by tolerating private acts of violence by young white thugs; and by the law enforcement practices of "the city's sheriff, Jim Clark, who dressed like George S. Patton and, with a private posse at his beck and call, ruled with an iron fist." One of Clark's tactics was to use cattle prods to disperse black attempts to organize peaceful demonstrations. The account of Lafayette's activities also explains how, despite his false arrest for vagrancy and his brutal beating, he succeeded in inspiring local support for black resistance to white misrule. By the end of the summer, he was organizing weekly mass meetings attended by over eight hundred protesters.

FBI [Federal Bureau of Investigation] agents monitored those meetings without providing Lafayette with any special support or protection. (Indeed, the FBI appears to have been more interested in assembling adverse information about Martin Luther King Jr. than in the safety of his followers.) They noted that much of Lafayette's support came from teenagers too young to vote. In his early organizing efforts, one important obstacle that he had to overcome was the concern of the older and more conservative members of the black community, including religious leaders, about the consequences of the white majority's reaction to the movement.

Following the example set by Lafayette in Selma, in 1963 in Birmingham, King also relied on the city's high school and even grammar school students for help in mobilizing large demonstrations. Responding to a demonstration on May 3, the notorious [Eugene] "Bull" Connor, May writes,

> let loose his police. They beat black youths with their nightsticks and allowed their vicious attack dogs to leap and bite the demonstrators, tearing their clothes and flesh. Then came the city's fire hoses that, when turned on, swept people away under streams of pressurized water. The protestors rolled and tumbled like rag dolls; among them was Colia Lafayette, whose injuries would incapacitate her for several months. After the assaults, came more arrests. By the end of the day over nine hundred children were in jail.

The Klan's response to King's demonstrations was even more vicious. On Sunday, September 15, 1963, presumably responding to King's famous "I Have a Dream" speech in Washington in August, Klansmen bombed the 16th Street Baptist Church in Birmingham, killing four girls instantly, and precipitating additional violence that caused other deaths and severe injuries. Those incidents motivated the administration of President John F. Kennedy to seek federal legislation that would curb such violence.

I was surprised to learn from May that the proposals first advanced by the Kennedy administration, unlike the statute ultimately enacted under Johnson's administration, would have limited the protection for the voting rights of blacks to those with a sixth-grade education. In response to Kennedy's proposal, King's followers "were furious. Southern states had prevented them from receiving an education equal to that of whites, and now they were being 'punished' for that denial at the ballot box."

The Edmund Pettus Bridge

Best known of the events in 1965 that finally led to the enactment of the VRA was the confrontation on the Edmund Pettus Bridge on March 7—a date that would become known as

The Last Actor Emancipation

An American citizen voting—surely there is nothing re-markable about that. But for an African American living in the Deep South in the 1960s, . . . it was a forbidden act, a dangerous act. There were nearly impossible ob-stacles to overcome: poll taxes, literacy tests, and hostile registrars. If a person succeeded and was allowed to vote, his name was published in the local newspaper, alerting his employers and others equally determined to stop him. The black men and women who dared to vote lost their jobs, their homes, and, often, their lives.

And yet they persevered. They marched on county courthouses, confronted sheriffs, and went to jail. In Selma, Alabama, on March 7, 1965, a day remembered as Bloody Sunday, they endured a brutal attack from state troopers and local vigilantes. That event touched the conscience of the nation, forcing President Lyndon B. Johnson to place a voting rights bill at the forefront of his political agenda. Its passage permitted millions of Af-rican Americans to vote in Alabama and elsewhere in the South. The Voting Rights Act transformed American de-mocracy and in many ways was the last act or emancipa-tion, a process Abraham Lincoln began in 1863.

Gary May,
Bending Toward Justice: The Voting Rights Act
and the Transformation of American Democracy.
New York: Basic Books, 2013.

"Bloody Sunday"—between six hundred men, women, and children who intended to march from Selma to Montgomery and helmeted Alabama law enforcement personnel armed with nightsticks, whips, and cattle prods, as well as firearms and tear gas. May describes how the police initiated their brutal attacks on the marchers, and the fact that the event was witnessed by newsmen from ABC, NBC, and CBS. National publicity generated significant support for the marchers. In her dissent in the recent Supreme Court case, Justice Ginsburg cites May's book and refers to those beatings as "the catalyst for the VRA's enactment."

Her characterization of "Bloody Sunday" as the "catalyst" is supported by May. After quoting a remark made by King a few days earlier—"We will write the voting right law in the streets of Selma"—May pointed out that King was wrong because, in May's words, "the Voting Rights Act would be written—in blood—on the Edmund Pettus Bridge." In fact, however, during the next few days President Johnson reacted unfavorably to numerous requests for immediate action, stating that he would not be "'blackjacked' into hasty action, whether it was sending troops to Selma or sending a voting rights bill to Congress."

Then, on Saturday, March 13, 1965 (just six days after "Bloody Sunday"), he met with Alabama's racist governor George Wallace in the Oval Office of the White House for over three hours. Wallace's insistence that he did not have the power to make it possible for blacks to vote in Alabama obviously offended and angered Johnson—as illustrated by the profane language that Johnson used in response—and may well have been the real catalyst that motivated prompt and decisive action by the president.

Later that Saturday, Johnson held a special press conference with over a hundred reporters:

He was no longer the indecisive, hesitant leader who had met with the clergymen just a few days prior. . . . He surprised reporters by announcing that a new voting rights bill would be sent to Congress on Monday, March 15—just two days away.

May's description of the events that occurred over that weekend, culminating in Johnson's eloquent speech to Congress on that Monday evening, makes it pellucidly clear that the president had finally concluded that there was an imperative need for prompt federal intervention to protect the voting rights of blacks.

In the prologue to his book, May identifies two important consequences of the VRA: it ended a half century of practices that prevented African Americans from exercising their right to vote, "and it transformed American politics by turning a once-solid Democratic South into a Republican stronghold." With respect to the first consequence, he expresses concern that even though the circumstances that gave birth to the act may not have an exact parallel today, their echoes can be found in more subtle and insidious efforts to prevent blacks from voting. He describes his concerns at length in the final chapter of his book where he criticizes photo ID laws and notes that an analysis of [Barack] Obama's election demonstrates that race remains a divisive issue—pointing to the fact that in Alabama in 2008 Obama received only 10 percent of the white vote.

With respect to the second consequence, May says very little; indeed, when I read that passage I questioned its accuracy, because during Reconstruction the former slaves voted overwhelmingly for Republican candidates and so one would expect that protecting their right to vote would benefit that party. It is not, however, an increase in the number of Republican blacks that turned the South into a Republican stronghold—because today most blacks vote for Democratic candidates. Instead, the Republican Party in the South has become more attractive to white voters who include the heirs of the white supremacists who were Democrats during and after Reconstruction.

Congress, Not the Court

The statistics set forth in Roberts's recent opinion persuasively explain why a neutral decision maker could reasonably conclude that at long last the imposition of the preclearance requirement on the states that lost the Civil War—or more precisely continuing to use the formula that in 1965 identified those states—is not justified by the conditions that prevail today. The opinion fails, however, to explain why such a decision should be made by the members of the Supreme Court. The members of Congress, representing the millions of voters who elected them, are far more likely to evaluate correctly the risk that the interest in maintaining the supremacy of the white race still plays a significant role in the politics of those states. After all, that interest was responsible for creating the slave bonus when the Constitution was framed, and in motivating the violent behavior that denied blacks access to the polls in those states for decades prior to the enactment of the VRA.

The several congressional decisions to preserve the preclearance requirement—including its 2006 decision—were preceded by thorough evidentiary hearings that have consistently disclosed more voting violations in those states than in other parts of the country. Those decisions have had the support of strong majority votes by members of both major political parties. Not only is Congress better able to evaluate the issue than the court, but it is also the branch of government designated by the Fifteenth Amendment to make decisions of this kind.

In her eloquent thirty-seven-page dissent, Justice Ginsburg, joined by Justices [Stephen] Breyer, [Sonia] Sotomayor, and [Elena] Kagan, described the extensive deliberations in Congress over the preclearance requirement, the precedents holding that the court has a duty to respect Congress's decisions, and the reasons why the preclearance remedy should be preserved. Indeed, she captured the majority's principal error concisely and clearly when she explained that "throwing out preclearance when it has worked and is continuing to work to stop discriminatory changes is like throwing away your umbrella in a rainstorm because you are not getting wet." Justice Ginsburg's conclusion sums up exactly why the VRA reauthorization should have been upheld:

> The record supporting the 2006 reauthorization of the VRA is . . . extraordinary. It was described by the chairman of the House Judiciary Committee as "one of the most extensive considerations of any piece of legislation that the United States Congress has dealt with in the 27½ years" he had served in the House. . . . After exhaustive evidence-gathering and deliberative process, Congress reauthorized the VRA, including the coverage provision, with overwhelming bipartisan support. It was the judgment of Congress that "40 years has not been a sufficient amount of time to eliminate the vestiges of discrimination following nearly 100 years of disregard for the dictates of the 15th Amendment and to ensure that the right of all citizens to vote is protected as guaranteed by the Constitution." . . . That determination of the body empowered to enforce the Civil War amendments "by appropriate legislation" merits this court's utmost respect. In my judgment, the court errs egregiously by overriding Congress's decision.

> *"Do you want to make it easier or harder for people to vote? The question, and answer, is really that simple."*

The Congressional Voting Rights Amendment Act Is Vital

Ari Berman

Ari Berman is a contributing writer for the Nation *and an investigative journalism fellow at the Nation Institute. In the following viewpoint, he reports on efforts in Congress to pass a bill, the Voting Rights Amendment Act, to restore some of the protections of the Voting Rights Act that the Supreme Court struck down. Berman says that the new law is not ideal and that it will not restrict voter identification (ID) laws, which have been one way states have worked to limit voting recently. He says that it is, however, a good step forward and makes it easier to challenge discriminatory voting policies in court. He argues that the bill should be passed as soon as possible.*

As you read, consider the following questions:

1. According to Berman, why does Section 5 of the VRA become a zombie without Section 4?

Ari Berman, "Members of Congress Introduce a New Fix for the Voting Rights Act," Reprinted with permission from the January 16, 2014 issue of *The Nation*. For subscription information, call 1-800-333-8536. Portions of each week's Nation magazine can be accessed at http://www.thenation.com.

2. Why does Berman say that voter ID laws have not been included in the new amendment to the VRA?

3. Why does Jim Sensenbrenner have credibility on voting rights issues, according to Berman?

Today Representatives Jim Sensenbrenner (R-WI) and John Conyers (D-MI) and Senator Patrick Leahy (D-VT) introduced legislation to strengthen the Voting Rights Act [VRA] of 1965 in the wake of the Supreme Court's decision last June [2013] invalidating a critical section of the VRA. The legislation, known as "the Voting Rights Amendment Act of 2014," represents the first attempt by a bipartisan group in Congress to reinstate the vital protections of the VRA that the Supreme Court took away.

Protecting Voting Rights

In the *Shelby County v. Holder* ruling on June 25, 2013, the court's conservative majority struck down Section 4 of the VRA, the formula that compelled specific states with a well-documented history of voting discrimination to clear their voting changes with the federal government under Section 5 of the VRA. The two provisions were always meant to work together; without Section 4, Section 5 became a zombie, applying to zero states.

Section 4 covered nine states (Alabama, Alaska, Arizona, Georgia, Louisiana, Mississippi, South Carolina, Texas and Virginia) and parts of six others (in California, Florida, Michigan, New York, North Carolina, South Dakota) based on evidence of voting discrimination against blacks and other minority groups dating back to the 1960s and 1970s. Since the *Shelby* decision, eight states previously covered under Section 4 have passed or implemented new voting restrictions. This includes onerous new laws in states like North Carolina and Texas, which the Justice Department objected to under other provisions of the VRA (Sections 2 and 3).

The Sensenbrenner-Conyers-Leahy bill strengthens the VRA in five distinct ways.

1: The legislation draws a new coverage formula for Section 4, thereby resurrecting Section 5. States with five violations of federal law to their voting changes over the past fifteen years will have to submit future election changes for federal approval. This new formula would currently apply to Georgia, Louisiana, Mississippi and Texas. Local jurisdictions would be covered if they commit three or more violations or have one violation and "persistent, extremely low minority turnout" over the past fifteen years.

The formula is based on a rolling calendar, updated with a current fifteen-year time period to exempt states who are no longer discriminating or add new ones who are, creating a deterrent against future voting rights violations. It's based on empirical conditions and current data, not geography or a fixed time period—which voting rights advocates hope will satisfy Chief Justice John Roberts should the new legislation be enacted and reach the Supreme Court.

The new Section 4 proposal is far from perfect. It does not apply to states with an extensive record of voting discrimination, like Alabama (where civil rights protests in Selma gave birth to the VRA), Arizona, Florida, North Carolina, South Carolina and Virginia, which were previously subject to Section 5. Nor does it apply to states like Ohio, Pennsylvania and Wisconsin that have enacted new voting restrictions in the past few years.

Moreover, Department of Justice objections to voter ID laws will not count as a new violation. Voter ID laws can still be blocked by DOJ [Department of Justice] in the new states covered under Section 4, but that will not be included as one of the five violations needed to keep the state covered. This exemption for voter ID laws was written to win the support of House majority leader Eric Cantor and other Republicans. [UPDATE: The preceding paragraphs were updated to reflect a correction. DOJ objections against voter ID laws will not count as a new violation, but federal court judgments will. So, from a voting rights perspective, this exemption is not as bad as previously reported.]

Section 3

2: The legislation strengthens Section 3 of the VRA, which has been described as the act's "secret weapon." Under Section 3, jurisdictions not covered by Section 4 could be "bailed-in" to federal supervision, but plaintiffs had to show evidence of intentional voting discrimination, which is very difficult to do in court. Under the new Section 3 proposal, any violation of the VRA or federal voting rights law—whether intentional or not—can be grounds for a bail-in, which will make it far easier to cover new states. (One major caveat, again, is that court objections to voter ID laws that are not found to be intentionally discriminatory cannot be used as grounds for "bail-in" under Section 3.)

3: The legislation mandates that jurisdictions in all fifty states have to provide notice in the local media and online of any election procedures related to redistricting, changes within 180 days of a federal election and the moving of a polling place. This will make it easier for citizens to identify potentially harmful voting changes in the forty-six states not subject to Sections 4 and 5.

4: The legislation makes it easier to seek a preliminary injunction against a potentially discriminatory voting law. Plaintiffs will now only have to show that the hardship to them outweighs the hardship to the state if a law is blocked in court pending a full trial. There will be a preliminary injunction hearing on North Carolina's voting law in July 2014, before the full trial takes place July 2015.

5: The legislation reaffirms that the attorney general [AG] can send federal observers to monitor elections in states subject to Section 4 and expands the AG's authority to send observers to jurisdictions with a history of discriminating against language minority groups, which includes parts of twenty-five states.

New Tools

The bill is certain to have its critics, including on the left. Voting rights supporters will argue, justifiably, that the new Section 4 formula does not apply to enough states and wrongly treats voter ID laws differently than other discriminatory voting changes. Despite these flaws, the legislation represents a significant improvement over the disastrous post-*Shelby* status quo, which has seen states like North Carolina and Texas rush to pass or implement blatantly discriminatory voting restrictions after being freed from federal oversight. The legislation strengthens voting rights protections in a number of tangible ways and gives the federal government and voting rights advocates new tools to combat voting discrimination.

The sponsors of the bill have a lot of credibility on this issue. Sensenbrenner, as chairman of the House Judiciary Committee, shepherded through the 2006 reauthorization of the VRA—which passed 390–33 in the House and 98–0 in the Senate. Conyers first entered Congress in 1965, the year of the VRA's passage, and has served on the House Judiciary Committee ever since. Leahy is chairman of the Senate Judiciary Committee and has recently worked with Sensenbrenner on reforming the NSA [National Security Agency].

The problem of contemporary voting discrimination ultimately requires a solution that only Congress can provide. It was Congress, after all, that passed the VRA in 1965 in response to the failure of litigation to stop the mass disenfranchisement of black voters in the South. Yes, yes, I realize that a Congress that can scarcely do more than name a Post Office nowadays is not likely to resurrect the VRA any time soon— especially when so much of the GOP [Grand Old Party, another name for Republicans] is devoted to erecting new barriers to the ballot box. But now that there's legislation on the table, members of Congress face a choice: Do you want to make it easier or harder for people to vote? The question, and answer, is really that simple.

▌ *"It is 2014, not 1965."*

The Congressional Voting Rights Amendment Act Is a Bad Idea

Hans A. von Spakovsky

Hans A. von Spakovsky is a senior legal fellow in the Heritage Foundation's Edwin Meese III Center for Legal and Judicial Studies. In the following viewpoint, he argues that the Voting Rights Amendment Act being considered in Congress is unconstitutional and discriminatory. He argues that, even with the Supreme Court's invalidation of parts of the Voting Rights Act, the Justice Department has explicit authority to prosecute any intentional discrimination against minorities. He says that the Voting Rights Amendment Act alters the law so that simple low voter turnout among minority voters, whatever the cause, will result in sanctions, which he says is unfair and unconstitutional. He concludes that the real goal of the legislation is to protect Democratic politicians, not to ensure racial fairness.

As you read, consider the following questions:

1. According to the author, what does Section 2 of the Voting Rights Act do?

2. Low turnout among which voters would not violate the Voting Rights Amendment Act, according to the author, and why does he say that this is a problem?

3. What example does the author provide of an instance in which voting rights law was used to protect Democrats?

In reaction to the U.S. Supreme Court's *Shelby County v. Holder* decision last June [2013], Rep. Jim Sensenbrenner (R., Wis.) and Sen. Patrick Leahy (D., Vt.) have introduced the Voting Rights Amendment Act of 2014. The stated purpose is to prevent racial discrimination. But what it would really do is force racial gerrymandering, make race the predominant factor in the election process, and advance the partisan interests of one political party.

Unconstitutional Overreach

Before *Shelby County*, Section 5 of the Voting Rights Act required certain states to get "preclearance" from the federal government before making any voting changes. But the Supreme Court ruled that the formula to determine which jurisdictions were covered was unconstitutional because it was based on 40-year-old turnout data that did not reflect contemporary conditions. Census Bureau data show that black-voter turnout is on par with or exceeds that of white voters in many of the formerly covered states and is higher than the rest of the country. We simply don't need Section 5 anymore.

The Supreme Court's ruling did not affect other provisions of the Voting Rights Act that protect voters, and the Justice Department and civil rights groups have been aggressively using them since *Shelby County*. All that's different now is that they must prove their case—as they must under any other civil rights law.

In particular there is Section 2, a permanent, nationwide ban on racial discrimination in voting. Section 2 bans not just intentional discrimination: It was expanded in 1982 to prohibit discriminatory "results" as well.

Further, Section 3 of the act allows a court to impose a preclearance requirement in a particular jurisdiction where a court determines that there is intentional misconduct, a much more reasonable and fair provision than the blanket requirements of Section 5.

But the bill would change Section 3 from requiring a showing of intentional discrimination to allowing other violations of the Voting Rights Act—most of which require only a showing of "disparate impact"—to count toward triggering preclearance coverage.

The Constitution, however, prohibits only intentional discrimination, and so that is the only reason Congress can impose the extraordinary preclearance regime. Obviously, showing that a government in one case has merely "violated" the statistical disparate impact test does not show that the government is likely to engage in unconstitutional violations. Once again, Congress is exceeding its constitutional bounds.

What's more, under the proposed bill "extremely low minority turnout" would be considered a "voting rights violation" that would count toward triggering preclearance, even if a jurisdiction engages in no discriminatory conduct. While low turnout might have been a plausible indicator of racial disenfranchisement in 1964, it is not plausible today.

Even worse, under the bill, low turnout by white voters would not count as a violation, even if they are a minority of voters in the district. If adopted, this would mark the first time that the Voting Rights Act actually excluded some Americans from protection based on their race.

Unfairly Helping Democrats

Other violations triggering coverage would include "objections" filed by the U.S. attorney general, which don't require any finding of intentional discrimination. A discriminatory effect based on statistical disparity is sufficient—"disparate impact" once again.

This is especially galling given the many past court decisions castigating the Justice Department for filing unwarranted objections under Section 5. In 2012, a federal court overturned Attorney General Eric Holder's objection to South Carolina's voter ID law—but it cost the state $3.5 million to beat the Justice Department. Most jurisdictions don't have the resources to fight the department.

Because tallying up rulings against a jurisdiction will trigger coverage, Mr. Holder and outside groups will have every incentive to file as many objections as possible and manufacture vexatious litigation. The triggers are so low (depending on the size of the jurisdiction, ranging from five to three to one so-called "voting-rights violations") that just about any place in the U.S. could be targeted.

Worse still, being placed into federal receivership will encourage racial and political gerrymanders. The 2006 changes to Section 5 imposed a "quota floor" for minority political success, prohibiting changes that "diminish the ability" of racial minorities to elect their "candidate of choice." This not only grants constitutionally problematic, racially preferential treatment to minorities, it skews the political playing field by preferring Democratic Party candidates.

For example, in 2012 a Texas court protected the district of white Democrat Rep. Lloyd Doggett, even though whites constitute the vast majority of voters in his district. It interpreted Section 5 to prohibit diminishing the electoral fortunes of white Democrats because they receive the support of most minority voters.

The bill also imposes burdensome and impractical information-disclosure requirements on local officials, such as providing demographic analysis of every precinct. Finally, the bill creates a novel legal standard for injunctive relief unknown in modern jurisprudence, inserting factors such as a "hardship" determination that favor plaintiffs' lawyers and virtually guarantee an injunction.

It is 2014, not 1965. This bill really isn't about the *Shelby County* decision. It is about having the federal government manipulate election rules to propagate racial gerrymandering and guarantee success for Democratic candidates. It would make race a predominant issue in election administration, instead of what its goal should be—making sure every eligible voter is able to vote, regardless of race.

"Racial discrimination continues to be a problem in our country, particularly in Section 5–covered states."

Section 5 of the Voting Rights Act Is Vital

Sandhya Bathija

Sandhya Bathija is a campaign manager with Legal Progress at the Center for American Progress. In the following viewpoint, she argues that Section 5 of the Voting Rights Act is vital to protect minority rights. Section 5 requires certain states to receive pre-clearance before they can change voting laws. Bathija says this is necessary given the ongoing examples of certain states passing discriminatory laws and attempting to reduce minority voting. Challenging such laws through litigation would be prohibitively expensive; however, she says, Section 5 allows the Justice Department to reject them without suing. She concludes that Section 5 has substantially advanced racial equality and justice in the United States.

As you read, consider the following questions:

1. What does Bathija say would have happened in Mississippi in 1997 without Section 5?

2. For what offices does Bathija say African Americans are still underrepresented?

3. According to the viewpoint, what is the purpose of federal observers, and how many were sent by the attorney general between 1996 and 2004?

On February 27 [2013] the U.S. Supreme Court will hear arguments in the case *Shelby County v. Holder*, a challenge to the constitutionality of Section 5 of the Voting Rights Act of 1965. This landmark law outlawed discriminatory voting practices by ending the disenfranchisement of minority voters and preventing vote dilution through racial gerrymandering and other techniques that negate the minority vote when the white majority votes as a bloc.

Section 5 furthers these goals by requiring nine full states and parts of six other states with a history of racial discrimination in voting to ask either the Department of Justice or a three-judge court in Washington, D.C., for approval before making any changes to voting laws—a process known as preclearance. Congress determined the jurisdictions originally covered under Section 5 by using a plan laid out in the Voting Rights Act and also created a scheme for states to "bail out" of coverage if they have complied with the Voting Rights Act for 10 years.

Here are five reasons why Section 5, by protecting the right to vote, actually enhances our democracy and is good for all Americans.

1. Section 5 Blocks Discriminatory Voting Practices

Section 5 has blocked discriminatory state laws that would have disenfranchised or diluted the minority vote. Without Section 5:

- Texas would have passed the strictest voter ID [identification] law in the nation in 2011, placing unforgiving burdens on minority voters. The law would have allowed concealed handgun licenses to serve as a form of valid identification to vote, but would have rejected the use of a college ID or a state employee ID. Luckily, Section 5 blocked the law and saved African American and Latino voters from being disenfranchised in the 2012 election.

- Mississippi would have required people to register to vote twice: once for federal elections and once for state and local elections. Knowing that it is more difficult for minorities to overcome administrative barriers, this tactic would have resulted in diluting the minority vote in state and local elections. The Department of Justice, using Section 5, blocked the law in 1997.

- Georgia would have continued to use a voter verification program to check the citizenship status of every person seeking to register to vote. Because Georgia failed to receive Section 5 preclearance before implementing the law, evidence was obtained that made it clear that minority voters were being flagged at higher rates, requiring time-consuming additional steps to be taken to prove their citizenship. The Department of Justice denied preclearance for this law in 2009.

- Arizona would have implemented a redistricting plan that would have divided certain election districts so Latinos would no longer be the majority in those districts and would no longer be able to elect candidates of their choice to represent them. The Department of Justice denied preclearance for this law in 2002.

2. Section 5 Safeguards Local Elections

The elimination of Section 5 may have the most devastating consequences in small cities and communities where individuals are less likely to litigate discriminatory changes. Section 5 requires covered jurisdictions to submit requests for even minor changes at the local level and protects against discriminatory practices that would otherwise go unnoticed.

- In 2011 the Pitt County School District in North Carolina decided to reduce the number of school board members from 12 to 7 and shorten their terms in office. Section 5 blocked the change from going into effect after the Department of Justice determined that such a change would decrease representation of minority-preferred candidates on the school board.

- In Clinton, Mississippi, where 34 percent of the population is African American, the city proposed to its six-member council a redistricting plan that did not include a single ward where African American voters had the power to elect candidates of their choice. Racially polarized voting is still a problem in Mississippi, and the redistricting plan ensured there was no longer a majority African American ward. The Department of Justice found reliable evidence that the city had acted with a racially discriminatory purpose and blocked the change from going into effect in 2011.

3. Section 5 Prevents Discrimination Where Race Is Still a Barrier

Under the Voting Rights Act, jurisdictions that must seek preclearance have a history of racial discrimination in voting practices, and there is still evidence that racial discrimination is prevalent in Section 5–covered jurisdictions. Most of the states fully covered under Section 5 have the highest African American populations in the country, which should mean that African Americans are strongly represented in the government. But that is unfortunately not the case.

African Americans are still significantly underrepresented in state legislatures, in Congress, and in statewide offices such

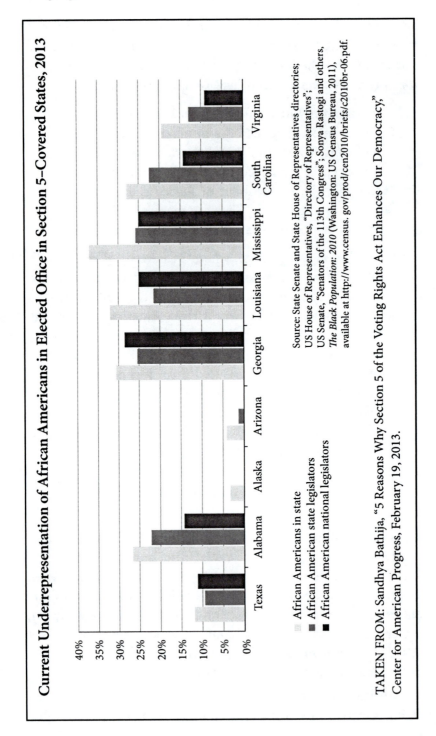

Current Underrepresentation of African Americans in Elected Office in Section 5–Covered States, 2013

- African Americans in state
- African American state legislators
- African American national legislators

Texas · Alabama · Alaska · Arizona · Georgia · Louisiana · Mississippi · South Carolina · Virginia

Source: State Senate and State House of Representatives directories; US House of Representatives, "Directory of Representatives"; US Senate, "Senators of the 113th Congress"; Sonya Rastogi and others, *The Black Population: 2010* (Washington: US Census Bureau, 2011), available at http://www.census. gov/prod/cen2010/briefs/c2010br-06.pdf.

TAKEN FROM: Sandhya Bathija, "5 Reasons Why Section 5 of the Voting Rights Act Enhances Our Democracy," Center for American Progress, February 19, 2013.

as governor and U.S. Senate positions. Where African Americans do serve in public office, they are elected in districts that are majority minority voters. Racially polarized voting such as this indicates that race is still a factor in how people vote.

- Mississippi, which is nearly 40 percent African American—the highest population of African Americans in any state in the country—has never elected an African American governor. There is one African American currently in Congress who represents Jackson, Mississippi, which is more than 60 percent African American.

- Louisiana, Mississippi, Virginia, Georgia, and South Carolina lead the country in being the most underrepresented when it comes to African Americans in the state legislature.

In addition, federal observers are frequently sent to Section 5–covered states on Election Day. The U.S. attorney general is permitted to send federal observers to certain Section 5–covered jurisdictions if there is reason to believe that voting rights will not be protected. Between 1966 and 2004, the attorney general sent a total of 1,142 federal observers to different states to monitor voting practices during elections. Most of these observers are sent into counties that are more than 40 percent nonwhite. Louisiana, Mississippi, Alabama, Georgia, and South Carolina accounted for 66 percent of all federal observer coverages between 1982 and 2004. When federal observers are sent to a jurisdiction, it is referred to as an "observer coverage." In the 2012 presidential election, the Department of Justice sent observers into counties in all of the fully covered Section 5 states except Virginia.

4. Section 5 Is a Necessary Alternative to Costly, Time-Intensive Litigation

Congress passed the Voting Rights Act because case-by-case litigation was not working to protect the right to vote in states where racial and ethnic discrimination mostly occurred. It was slow, difficult, and costly to challenge every type of voter suppression tactic used in counties and states around the country. And even when litigation was successful in stopping the unconstitutional practices, state officials would ignore the court orders or find some new discriminatory scheme to ensure minorities could not exercise their right to vote.

This would not be any different today. Consider the number of states that passed voter suppression laws since 2010 in Section 5–covered jurisdictions. Without Section 5, minority voters would have had to build a case, front the costs, and challenge the following laws:

- Proof-of-citizenship laws: Alabama, Arizona, and Georgia

- Voter ID laws: Alabama, Mississippi, South Carolina, and Texas—in fact, because of Section 5, South Carolina watered down its original version of the law before seeking approval from the U.S. District Court for the District of Columbia

- Limits to early voting: Georgia

- Instead, Section 5 required the Justice Department or the D.C. Circuit Court to approve the laws before they disenfranchised minority voters.

5. Section 5 Has Moved Our Country Forward

Thanks to the Voting Rights Act and Section 5, the United States has made immense progress in protecting and expanding the right to vote. In Section 5–covered jurisdictions, change is happening, although slowly, but it may not have happened at all if it were not for the Voting Rights Act and Section 5. The changes we see include:

- The election of the first African American president

- A higher percentage of African American elected officials—the number of which has increased from just 300 nationwide in 1964 to more than 9,100 today

- The highest ever percentage of African Americans in Mississippi's state legislature—27 percent—since the first African American to Mississippi's state legislature was elected in 1967, following the passage of the Voting Rights Act

- A more diverse electorate

Racial discrimination continues to be a problem in our country, particularly in Section 5–covered states. Section 5 serves as a shield to protect minority voters in jurisdictions where progress has come slowly and continues to be a necessary remedy to disenfranchisement. Without it, minority voters would be in jeopardy—and so too would our democracy.

Periodical and Internet Sources Bibliography

The following articles have been selected to supplement the diverse views presented in this chapter.

Ari Berman	"Republicans Used to Support Voting Rights—What Happened?," *Nation*, April 14, 2014.
Matthew Cooper	"Voting Rights Act Faces a Supreme Test," *National Journal*, February 14, 2013.
Jaime Fuller	"Why Voting Rights Is the Democrats' Most Important Project in 2014," *Washington Post*, April 10, 2014.
Dylan Matthews	"Here's How Congress Could Fix the Voting Rights Act," *Washington Post*, June 25, 2013.
Gary May	"Over 48 Years, GOP Strays Far from Voting Rights," *CNN*, August 7, 2013.
New York Times	"A Step Toward Restoring Voting Rights," January 18, 2014.
Eyder Peralta, Scott Neuman, and Mark Memmott	"Supreme Court Strikes Down Key Provision of Voting Rights Law," *NPR*, June 25, 2013.
Philip Rucker	"Clinton Defends Voting Rights Act, Says States Revive 'Old Demons of Discrimination,'" *Washington Post*, August 12, 2013.
Washington Post	"Voting Rights Act Should Be Revived by Congress, Not by Justice Suing States," October 6, 2013.
DeWayne Wickham	"Voting Rights Get Bipartisan Boost," *USA Today*, January 21, 2014.
Richard Wolf	"On March's Anniversary, Voting Rights Still an Issue," *USA Today*, August 25, 2013.

OPPOSING
VIEWPOINTS®
SERIES

Are States Restricting Voting Rights?

Chapter Preface

In 2011 Wisconsin passed a law requiring voters to show photo identification (ID) at their polling place in order to be allowed to cast their ballots. The law was presented as a way to ensure against voter fraud.

However, in early 2014, federal judge Lynn Adelman struck down the law as unconstitutional and discriminatory. Adelman agreed with plaintiffs, who had argued that the law would disproportionately affect minority and poor voters, many of whom would not be able to get access to voter ID and would therefore be disenfranchised. Moreover, Adelman concluded that the fear of voting fraud was overstated and inaccurate. As quoted by Andrew Cohen in an April 30, 2014, article in the *Atlantic*, Adelman said,

> In the present case, no evidence suggests that voter-impersonation fraud will become a problem at any time in the foreseeable future. As the plaintiffs' unrebutted evidence shows, a person would have to be insane to commit voter-impersonation fraud. The potential costs of perpetrating the fraud, which include a $10,000 fine and three years of imprisonment, are extremely high in comparison to the potential benefits, which would be nothing more than one additional vote for a preferred candidate (or one fewer vote for an opposing candidate), a vote which is unlikely to change the election's outcome.

Jamelle Bouie writing for *Slate* in an April 30, 2014, post celebrates the verdict and explains that "this ruling is significant for more than what it means for Wisconsin. As Ari Berman notes for the *Nation*, it's part of a larger trend of courts striking down voter identification laws. In the last year, four other states—Arkansas, Pennsylvania, Missouri, and Texas—have had their requirements reversed by federal courts."

Other commenters, however, thought that the verdict was unfair and misguided. For instance, Hans A. von Spakovsky in a May 2, 2014, article at *National Review Online* argues that the Supreme Court had already ruled that voter ID laws such as those in Wisconsin did not place an undue burden on voters, since Wisconsin provides free IDs. Spakovsky adds that "Judge Adelman summarily dismissed the rationales that Wisconsin put forward to justify its voter-ID law—the same rationales the Supreme Court concluded in *Crawford* [referring to 2008's *Crawford v. Marion County Election Board*] were legitimate legislative concerns." Spakovsky argues, then, that the Supreme Court has already made voter ID laws legitimate and that Adelman was going against established precedent to arrive at an illegitimate verdict.

The authors in the following chapter examine voting restriction controversies in other states, including Texas, North Carolina, and Pennsylvania.

> "But the North Carolina legislature, with a new united Republican legislature and governor, went further and passed the mother of all voter suppression bills."

Supreme Error

Richard L. Hasen

Richard L. Hasen is a professor of law and political science at the University of California, Irvine School of Law. In the following viewpoint, he reports that North Carolina has passed sweeping voter laws that will restrict people's ability to vote and will especially affect minority voters. Hasen says that these laws would never have passed if the Supreme Court had not struck down an important provision of the Voting Rights Act. The new laws show that the Voting Rights Act provision was necessary, he argues, and illustrate that the court was wrong when it argued that the provision was no longer needed.

As you read, consider the following questions:

1. According to Hasen, what did Chief Justice John Roberts mean when he compared the Voting Rights Act to an elephant whistle?

2. List two restrictive provisions of the North Carolina voting law as stated in the viewpoint.

3. What group is North Carolina allowed to discriminate against under current law, according to Hasen?

Usually it takes years to judge when the Supreme Court gets something very wrong. Think of Justice [Anthony] Kennedy's opinion for the court in the 2010 campaign-finance case, *Citizens United [v. Federal Election Commission]*, freeing corporations to spend money on elections. He wrote that the "appearance of [corporate] influence or access will not cause the electorate to lose faith in our democracy," a point that remains hotly debated even as the amount of money in federal elections skyrockets.

Voting Rights Act Is Needed

But the conservative justices' decision this past June [2013] in *Shelby County v. Holder*, striking down a key provision of the Voting Rights Act, has already unleashed in North Carolina the most restrictive voting law we've seen since the 1965 enactment of the VRA. Texas is restoring its voter ID law which had been blocked (pursuant to the VRA) by the federal government. And more is to come in other states dominated by Republican legislatures. Substituting their own judgment for that of Congress, the five justices in the *Shelby County* majority expressed confidence that the act's "preclearance" provision was no longer necessary, and that there would be ample other tools to fight discrimination in voting. That the conservative justices have already been proven wrong a few scant weeks after the decision came down offers little solace for the voters of North Carolina, who ironically will have to try to fix the problem using the very mechanism of voting—which the North Carolina legislature is inhibiting.

Back in 2009, the court considered whether to strike down Congress's renewal of the rule requiring jurisdictions with a history of racial discrimination in voting to get federal approval before making changes in their voting laws. The feds had to withhold approval unless the covered jurisdictions demonstrated the law would *not* make minority voters worse off and was *not* motivated by an intention to do so.

During oral arguments in that 2009 case (which ultimately ducked the constitutional question), Chief Justice Roberts judged the law unnecessary, analogizing the federal approval requirement to an "elephant whistle." "You know, I have this whistle to keep away the elephants. You know, well, that's silly. Well, there are no elephants, so it must work."

Elephant Whistle and Live Elephants

Similarly, during arguments in the *Shelby County* case, Justice Kennedy opined that other provisions of the Voting Rights Act, especially Section 2, would still protect minority voters. The *Shelby County* opinion itself declared that "our decision in no way affects the permanent, nationwide ban on racial discrimination in voting found in §2." Congress, of course, had made a different judgment about the continuing deterrent effect of the need to obtain federal preclearance, and Justice [Ruth Bader] Ginsburg's dissent in *Shelby County* analogized chucking the preclearance regime to "throwing away your umbrella in a rainstorm because you are not getting wet." In a sense, the empirical question can be said to be whether the elephant whistle was never necessary; or the umbrella was working the whole time. It took only months to ascertain that the umbrella was probably working. Within two hours of the Supreme Court's issuance of its decision in *Shelby County*, formerly covered state Texas announced that it would now enforce its voter identification law (concealed weapons permit OK; student ID not), which had been blocked by both the Department of Justice and a federal court in Washington, D.C.

But the North Carolina legislature, with a new united Republican legislature and governor, went further and passed the

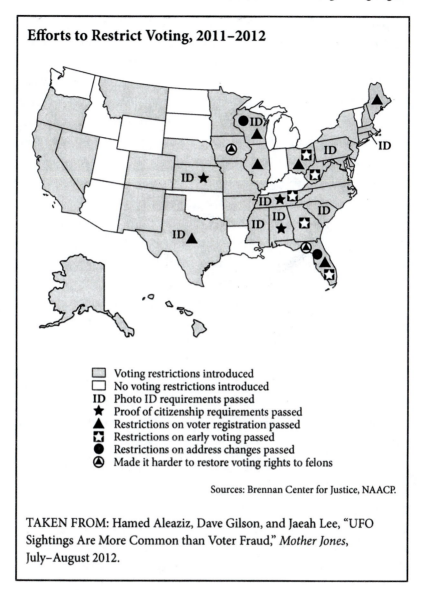

Efforts to Restrict Voting, 2011–2012

Voting restrictions introduced
No voting restrictions introduced
ID Photo ID requirements passed
★ Proof of citizenship requirements passed
▲ Restrictions on voter registration passed
✪ Restrictions on early voting passed
● Restrictions on address changes passed
Ⓐ Made it harder to restore voting rights to felons

Sources: Brennan Center for Justice, NAACP.

TAKEN FROM: Hamed Aleaziz, Dave Gilson, and Jaeah Lee, "UFO Sightings Are More Common than Voter Fraud," *Mother Jones*, July–August 2012.

mother of all voter suppression bills. Aside from enacting a strict voter ID law like Texas's, the bill also cut a week off early voting in the state (used by up to 70 percent of African American voters in 2012) and barred local election boards from keeping the polls open on the final Saturday before the election after 1 P.M. It eliminated same-day voter registration.

It opened up the precincts to "challengers" who can gum up the works at polling places and dissuade voters from showing up in the first place. It banned paying voter registration card circulators by the piece. It eliminated pre-registration of 16- and 17-year-olds in the high schools. And it said that a voter who votes in the wrong precinct (perhaps because of a poll worker's error) will have her whole ballot thrown out—earlier law had allowed such ballots to count for those races in which the voter was eligible to vote.

Forty of North Carolina's counties were covered by the preclearance requirement before *Shelby County*, and a draconian law like this would never have made it past the Justice Department. Nor would a whole bunch of local shenanigans deployed just last week in suppressing student and other voting. The Associated Press reported that "the Pasquotank County Board of Elections on Tuesday barred an Elizabeth City State University senior from running for city council, ruling his on-campus address couldn't be used to establish local residency. Following the decision, the head of the county's Republican Party said he plans to challenge the voter registrations of more students at the historically black university ahead of upcoming elections."

Pasquotank County used to be a covered jurisdiction.

It turns out the elephant whistle was really keeping away elephants, in the form of local Republican election officials on election boards, as Rachel Maddow's recent report shows. No problem, the *Shelby County* justices might say, just use all those other tools to fight racial discrimination in voting.

Discrimination

But not so fast. It turns out that thanks to the Supreme Court's ruling in various cases, these other tools are unlikely to work to challenge most provisions of the new North Carolina law. To begin with, if North Carolina can demonstrate that it is motivated in its election laws by an intent to discriminate against *Democrats* rather than on the basis of *race* (despite the high correlation between the two), many constitutional claims will fail for lack of proof of intentional racial discrimination. Texas has already made this argument in defending its redistricting that a federal court found to be the product of intentional race discrimination: "DOJ's accusations of racial discrimination are baseless. In 2011, both houses of the Texas legislature were controlled by large Republican majorities, and their redistricting decisions were designed to increase the Republican Party's electoral prospects at the expense of the Democrats. It is perfectly constitutional for a Republican-controlled legislature to make partisan districting decisions, even if there are incidental effects on minority voters who support Democratic candidates."

Further, the court has held that voter identification laws are generally constitutional, with a possible exception for voters who can demonstrate that the law imposes special burdens on them, despite a lack of evidence of impersonation fraud which could justify the law. As for Section 2, the other part of the Voting Rights Act that Justice Kennedy touted as a good substitute for the end of preclearance: There hasn't been a successful Section 2 challenge to voter id laws, and outside of redistricting cases the courts have read Section 2 very narrowly. And the chances are slim that the Department of Justice can prove enough intentional discrimination by North Carolina to get it "bailed in" to preclearance under another provision of the Voting Rights Act.

To be sure, some of these provisions likely will be found to violate the Constitution. Students have a constitutional right to register and vote where they go to school. The 6th Circuit has held that it is unconstitutional for Ohio to disenfranchise voters casting provisional ballots if they were sent to the wrong precinct because of voter error. A few other provisions are likely to fall too, maybe in state courts under the state constitution. But the main fight over these laws is going to have to be political, not legal. Dave Weigel and Ari Berman have been considering whether there will be enough political backlash to overcome these North Carolina shenanigans. But thanks to these very laws, it will take a lot of effort to get people to the polls casting valid votes to go against the laws. And that's part of the point.

It's enough to make one wonder whether the justices in the *Shelby County* majority actually thought minority voters would still have effective tools to fight discrimination after the justices struck Section 5, or if they suspected all along that a stampede of elephants was right around the corner.

"Voter fraud is real and always plausible."

North Carolina Is Protecting the Integrity of Voting

Mark H. Creech

Mark H. Creech is executive director of the Raleigh-based Christian Action League of North Carolina. In the following viewpoint, he argues that the new North Carolina elections laws are necessary. He says that North Carolina's election system was antiquated and confusing. Moreover, election fraud is always a possibility, and steps need to be taken to prevent it. Finally, he says that everyone should have a form of identification (ID), for voting and for many other purposes. He suggests that churches should have drives to ensure that everyone has an ID for Election Day.

As you read, consider the following questions:

1. According to Creech, how did Lyndon Johnson earn his nickname "Landslide Lyndon"?

2. According to Creech, how has one-stop early voting failed to live up to its promise?

3. What does Creech say is a Christian's most sacred civic duty?

North Carolina's new voter ID [identification] law came under assault last week [in March 2014] from Van Jones, a Democrat and host of CNN's *Crossfire*. During the broadcast, which featured North Carolina Gov. Pat McCrory as a guest, Jones said the new law was a means of rigging the state's election system and essentially suppressing the vote of African Americans, lower income people, and others who would vote against the state's Republican majority.

Voter Fraud

Jones's remarks reflect a common objection of Democrats, Moral Monday marchers, and even U.S. Attorney General Eric Holder. Under Holder's direction the Department of Justice has filed a suit against the state over the statute.

The new state law, however, is actually about protecting the integrity of the vote in the Tar Heel State. Voter fraud is real and always plausible.

Few people are aware or remember the way Lyndon Johnson [LBJ] acquired his ironic nickname, "Landslide Lyndon." LBJ earned the title in his 1948 bid for a U.S. Senate seat representing the Lone Star State. In that election, it appeared Johnson had lost. But just six days after Election Day, it was discovered in the precinct of Alice that 203 people voted at the last minute, making Johnson the winner. All except one had voted for Johnson. Strangely, however, the 203 people that voted had done so in alphabetical order. That seemed terribly suspicious to Johnson's opponent, Texas governor Coke Stevenson, who sued and won an injunction from the federal district court, barring Johnson from the general election ballot. But Supreme Court justice Hugo Black, who was a sitting circuit justice, ruled the federal court had no jurisdiction in the case and ordered the injunction stayed. Black's decision and Johnson's narrow win of 87 votes would later be upheld by the Supreme Court. It was only in 1977, four years after the late Johnson's passing, that an election judge in Alice admitted that he had helped rig the election.

Such examples provide the impetus for states to vigilantly revise, reform, and upgrade their election laws wherever necessary to protect the vote, which is exactly what North Carolina's current leadership did during the last session of the General Assembly. The legislation that passed not only addressed the need for valid voter identification, but also numerous other constructive provisions pertaining to the state's elections.

Before the new voter ID law, many of the state's election rules had become antiquated. They had largely been written for a time when voting occurred on one day (Election Day) in communities where most people knew the identity of the voter who walked in the polling place. But everyone knows that isn't the situation today—far from it.

Antiquated System

Over time, newer laws were added, many of them overlapping the old and making the state's election system too complicated.

For instance, the deadline to register to vote was 25 days before Election Day. That is, unless a person waited to register to vote during the early voting period when same-day registration was allowed. Then, one could register to vote and cast a ballot at the same time.

A second example is that in order to vote, the requirement was simply to announce one's name and address at the polls. That is, unless the registration was done by mail, then the first time one voted, it was necessary to show some form of identification. Those who registered to vote via same-day registration were also required to show an ID.

A third example was that all voters who registered or made changes to their registration were mailed verification forms to ensure that they actually lived where they claimed to reside. That is, unless the person registered during same-day registration, in which case there was no time to verify the voter's address.

What a convoluted mess; a mess that failed to effectively serve the North Carolina electorate with an election system beyond reproach, one that leveled the playing field for everyone.

A few years ago, when one-stop early voting was first pitched to the legislature, it was touted as a way to increase turnout, but it didn't work out that way. Early voting was convenient, but it only resulted in the same people who always turned out to vote casting their votes early. Voter turnout did intensify during early voting, mostly during presidential elections, but it didn't result in a larger general upsurge in voters for the election.

Problems with One-Stop Voting

Although the new law allows for the same number of hours to get to the polls as the last equivalent election, it shortens the time for voters to cast their ballots early during one-stop voting—and for good reason. One-stop early voting is problematic for the state's local election boards. Their responsibility requires making certain the poll books are updated with all absentee voters. Because early voting ends on the Saturday before Election Day, it can be impossible to do so before the polling places open on the day of the vote. The early-voting process can provide the greatest potential for fraud, if an ID is not required. What would stop a person from voting at an early voting site—as long as he could present a name and address from the voter rolls? The only thing necessary would be to visit the state Board of Elections web site and access the entire list of North Carolina voters' names and addresses.

Georgia and Vote Fraud

Georgia had actually implemented its first voter ID [identification] law for in-person voting in 1997 when Democrats controlled the state's legislature. It listed seventeen different documents that could be used, such as a birth certificate, Social Security card, current utility bill, government check, payroll check or bank statement, and it had an exemption that allowed a voter to complete an affidavit swearing to his identity instead of producing a document. A lawyer who worked as a lobbyist in Georgia and who was there when the law was passed told me that not only did black legislators insist on the affidavit exemption, but everyone knew that the [Bill] Clinton–controlled Justice Department would never approve an ID requirement without one.

Georgia had a history of disputed elections and fraudulent voting, including the infamous vote fraud that helped elect Herman Talmadge governor in 1947 when voters in places like Telfair County voted in alphabetical order or from their cemetery plots. Jimmy Carter was almost cheated out of his first election because of vote fraud by local political bosses. The dangers and threats to the security of elections were demonstrated by an analysis conducted by the *Atlanta Journal-Constitution* and WSB-TV, published in 2000, which found that more than 5,412 votes had been cast in the names of deceased voters in Georgia, sometimes on multiple occasions, over the prior twenty years, and at least 15,000 dead voters were still registered to vote.

John Fund, Stealing Elections:
How Voter Fraud Threatens Our Democracy.
New York: Encounter Books, 2008.

Moreover, employees for the various county boards of elections have reported receiving complaints from a voter or sometimes several voters, who would call and say they had gone to vote, only to learn that someone had already voted in their name. Sadly, the Board of Elections, both county and state, would excuse these reports simply as administrative error, and thus, allow the disenfranchised voter to cast a vote anyway and then have that vote count. What's really egregious, however, is the fact that it was impossible to know what really happened. It could only be surmised. Over time, North Carolina's voter laws had developed in such a way as to make fraud detection considerably difficult.

Of course, some will contend these allegations of voter fraud are just a lot of hoopla over nothing, but they aren't!

Citizens in Pasquotank County successfully removed more than 60 voters from their rolls after the 2012 election, but unfortunately, only when the votes had already been counted. The voters attested that they were residents at the local college, but that didn't prove to be true. It's impossible to know even if they lived in the county, but it's abundantly clear they didn't live at the addresses on their voter registration. That's definitely voter fraud and it is most naïve to think it isn't happening elsewhere in the state.

But even if there isn't widespread proof of voter fraud, isn't the very possibility of trickery—the alleging of voter deception—a matter to be vigorous in trying to prevent? This involves the most important right exercised as a citizen of a representative democracy—the right to vote!

If it were difficult to prove a claim that there was illegal street racing on a certain highway, would that be reason enough not to send the highway patrol to watch the area as a preventative measure—as a means of possibly saving lives?

The same reasonable principle should also apply to minimizing the potential for voter fraud.

Take Precautions

We should always assume voter fraud is possible and take precautions. Most of the electorate understands this; and no doubt, that is much of the reason why 70 to 80 percent of voters favor voter ID.

Still, there is one more reason to support North Carolina's voter ID law. It's the fact that everybody ought to have a valid ID—everyone. There are so many reasons one would need an ID: applying for a marriage license, entering many government buildings and courthouses, jury duty, applying for a job, applying for employment insurance, for doctors and dentists visits, to get a library card, to pick up a prescription or purchase some cold medication, to enroll a child in school, to rent a car or an apartment, to get a package from FedEx or UPS, to cash a check, and the list goes on. Everybody ought to have an ID!

How telling is the need for everyone to have a valid ID, when Moral Monday organizers, the loudest voice opposing the new voter ID law, called upon marchers participating in a recent rally in Raleigh to keep one on their person at all times? Go figure.

That being said, since a valid voter ID isn't required to vote in North Carolina until the 2016 election, churches need to engage in drives that help every citizen of the state to secure one. Fewer actions would be a better demonstration of obedience to Christ's command to render unto Caesar the things that belong to Caesar, and unto God the things that belong to God (Matthew 22:21).

For the Christian, voting is the most sacred of civic duties. People on the left may continue railing against the new voter ID law, but it only works to protect the integrity of the state's elections. And that's something that even pleases the Almighty.

"A state can't abridge important rights
just because it feels like it."

Why Pennsylvania's Voter ID Law Is Unconstitutional

Garrett Epps

Garrett Epps is a former reporter for the Washington Post, *a novelist, and a legal scholar. He teaches courses in constitutional law and creative writing at the University of Baltimore; his most recent book is* American Epic: Reading the U.S. Constitution. *In the following viewpoint, Epps argues that the Pennsylvania voter identification (ID) law is intended by Republicans to disenfranchise poor and minority voters. He says that the right to vote is fundamental and that Pennsylvania needs to show an important reason to abridge it. Pennsylvania has claimed that it needs the law to prevent fraud, but the state has not managed to show any evidence that fraud is actually a problem. He concludes that the voter ID law should therefore be viewed as unconstitutional.*

As you read, consider the following questions:

1. According to the viewpoint, what did Republican representative Mike Turzai say was the goal of the voter ID law in Pennsylvania?

2. What does "strict scrutiny" mean, according to Epps?

3. Where does the Constitution provide a guaranteed right to vote, according to Epps?

In time, *Crawford v. Marion County Election Board* may come to rank with *Bush v. Gore* as among the worst recent decisions by the Supreme Court. That case has made possible the ongoing campaign to gut the right to vote.

Crawford is directly responsible for Wednesday's decision by Pennsylvania state judge Robert Simpson to allow that state's strict voter ID law to take effect. That law is all but certain to cause chaos at some polling places this fall. It may also, according to some credible estimates, disfranchise as many as 9 percent of the state's eligible voters. There's little secret about the purpose of the bill. As the state's Republican House Majority Leader, Mike Turzai, told a partisan audience in June, it "is gonna allow Governor [Mitt] Romney to win the state of Pennsylvania."

None of these outcomes is certain, but what does seem certain is that some eligible voters in Pennsylvania will be unable to vote under the new rules. And all sides concede that there is no demonstrable need for the stricter ID rules. The bill's Republican sponsors originally raised the specter of voter fraud, but at trial the state conceded that there were no recorded reports of investigations into or prosecutions for voter impersonation on record anywhere in the state. Instead, the state argued that the law "improves the security and integrity of elections" because many other activities require government-issued ID as well.

This rationale is in essence empty. The government wants to impose a strict voter ID requirement because, well, it wants to. It's tidier. In some contexts where we require ID, such a justification is really fine. For example, requiring extensive documentation to obtain a cab driver's license is probably okay, even if there's no evidence of fraudulent cab driving.

That's because the right to a cab license isn't what constitutional lawyers call "fundamental."

But a state can't abridge important rights just because it feels like it. If the right to vote is important, then the state's justification is as sinister as if it decided to cut back on free speech because bureaucrats prefer the quiet.

The key issue in voting-rights cases is what "standard of scrutiny" the Constitution requires for burdens on the right to vote—that is, new rules that make it harder to cast a ballot without entirely banning any individual or group from voting. If the right to vote is fundamental, then the standard should be "strict scrutiny"; that means the government must show a very important reason before it is allowed to burden the right. "Security and integrity" might meet that test—but only if they face an actual threat. The state would have to produce evidence that fraud is actually likely to be a serious problem.

But Judge Simpson in his opinion claims that the Supreme Court's standard is a "deferential" one. Here he tips his ideological hand, because this standard is not law, but rather a creation of the court's three hardest right-wingers. Though proposed in a concurrence by Justice [Antonin] Scalia, the "deferential" standard was explicitly *rejected* in Justice [John Paul] Stevens's three-judge opinion announcing the judgment. Under Judge Simpson's extremist reading, however, no matter how strict the government regulation, challengers must prove that someone is *certain* to be disfranchised—an almost impossible standard to meet.

Simpson could have decided the case on state constitutional law grounds—the Pennsylvania Constitution provides that "[e]lections shall be free and equal; and no power, civil or military, shall at any time interfere to prevent the free exercise of the right of suffrage." But, like too many state courts around the country, he does not bother to give that clause an independent meaning, instead taking his cue from the right wing of the *Crawford* court.

The Real Vote Fraud

Howard L. Simon, executive director of the American Civil Liberties Union of Florida, examined how a new system of election malfeasance was being perpetrated around the country for the 2012 election season:

What is happening in more than two dozen states is that the claim of widespread voter fraud has been used as an excuse to make it more difficult to register to vote, to cast your vote, and to have your vote counted. That—rather than the chimera of widespread voting fraud—is the real threat to democracy. These laws are not intended to apply evenly. The voting restrictions enacted in Florida disproportionately impact minority groups, recently naturalized citizens, students, and people who need to get time off from their jobs to vote.

Another article in the *Washington Post* . . . noted that the new legislation might prevent up to ten million Hispanics from voting in November 2012—coincidentally, a population that was previewed to overwhelmingly support the Democratic candidate for president. Republican state legislatures passed *all* of the new laws restricting access to the polls, and the legislation targeted historically Democratic voting populations.

The irony, of course, is that if some of these exact same voter fraud methods were utilized in countries such as Iraq, Vietnam or Venezuela, [former secretary of state] Colin Powell, [former president] Jimmy Carter and the U.S. government would be sternly warning that the veracity of the vote would be called into question, and stating that to fully trust the results, the United States needed greater assurance of election credibility.

Thomas Block, Machiavelli in America.
New York: Algora Publishing, 2014.

To Americans, we often hear, the vote is a "privilege," not a right. That idea dates back to the early days of the Republic, when "democracy" was a swear word and the Constitution provided only that states could not restrict federal voting more strictly than voting in their own elections.

But since then, the Constitution has changed. Of all the textually guaranteed rights in the Constitution, "the right to vote" is mentioned most often—indeed, beginning in 1868, it has been reaffirmed no fewer than five times, in § 2 of the Fourteenth Amendment, § 1 of the Fifteenth Amendment, the Nineteenth Amendment, § 1 of the Twenty-Fourth Amendment, and § 1 of the Twenty-Sixth Amendment. (Look it up.)

It's true that none of these provisions says, "Every citizen has a fundamental right to vote, *and we ain't playing with you when we say that.*" Instead, they protect against specific grounds of abridgment. But no other right in the Constitution is spelled out that way either. Freedom of speech, freedom of the press, the "right to keep and bear arms"—these rights are also, in the same kind of language, assumed to exist and protected against state abridgment.

A modern democracy isn't worthy of the name unless it protects universal suffrage. That doesn't mean the state can't regulate voting—by requiring some forms of ID, for example. It simply means that when the state wants to make it harder to vote, it has to do exactly what it must do when it wants to make it harder to speak: show a very good, factual, neutral, not imaginary reason for doing so.

Despite the current fever for voter ID laws, no state has managed to do that. Proponents warn darkly of terrorists and illegal aliens overwhelming the polls, but when asked to show proof, they can't.

Pamela Karlan of Stanford Law School, one of the nation's leading voting rights litigators, reminded a Washington audience a few years ago of Justice Louis D. Brandeis's famous warning against fear. "Men feared witches and burnt women,"

Brandeis said in a famous dissent. After *Crawford,* among the first Indiana voters turned away from the polls was a group of nuns in their 80s and 90s.

"We fear terrorists and disfranchise nuns," Karlan said.

I grew up in a time and place where the "privilege" theory permitted my home state to impose poll taxes and literacy tests. As a result, an electoral winner sometimes had the support of as few as 10 percent of eligible voters.

Those restrictions were wrong because they had a racial motive, but they were also wrong because they were undemocratic.

Powerful forces today would like to carry us back to the time when the government doled out ballots to those it approved of. It will be an ill-omened voyage.

> *"It's not as if there aren't clues that voter fraud is a problem."*

Winning the Fight for Voter-ID

John Fund

John Fund is the national affairs columnist for National Review Online *and a senior editor at the* American Spectator. *In the following viewpoint, he argues that fraud is a long-term, serious problem in Philadelphia and that Pennsylvania is justified in passing a voter identification (ID) law to try to reduce illegality in elections. Fund adds that the Pennsylvania law was poorly implemented, and he argues that it is in everyone's interest to make sure elections are fair and to ensure that all citizens can obtain a voter ID.*

As you read, consider the following questions:

1. Why will the court case decided against the Pennsylvania voter ID law not affect similar laws in other states, according to Fund?

2. What personal experience of Arlen Specter does Fund believe may have led him to support voter ID laws?

3. In what ways is Mexico's election system superior to America's system, according to the viewpoint?

In 2008, the U.S. Supreme Court upheld on a 6-to-3 vote the constitutionality of laws requiring voter ID at the polls. Justice John Paul Stevens, one of the left-of-center judges on the court, wrote the opinion in a case involving Indiana's voter-ID law: He found that the court could not "conclude that the statute imposes 'excessively burdensome requirements' on any class of voters."

But our Constitution decentralizes our election procedures over 13,000 counties and towns, and states themselves are in charge of writing voter-ID laws should they choose to do so. Some do it better than others.

Last Friday, Judge Bernard McGinley of the Pennsylvania Commonwealth Court found that his state's voter-ID law violated Pennsylvania's constitution because the manner in which it was implemented placed an unreasonable burden on voters. The law, passed in 2012, had been blocked from taking effect while the court case against it ground forward. McGinley's decision is likely to be appealed to the Pennsylvania Supreme Court. Or the legislature could pass a new version of the law that would answer the judge's objections.

McGinley concluded that the law had been implemented in a sloppy, haphazard way and that the state had not done enough to help provide IDs to voters who lacked one. Opponents of voter-ID laws are cheering the Pennsylvania ruling as a harbinger of further rollback of such laws nationwide. But it's hardly that. "The relevance of this ruling to other voter ID challenges is somewhat limited," writes Rick Hasen, a law professor specializing in election law at the University of California at Irvine. "The findings on implementation are state specific and don't really carry over to other states."

In addition, the judge found that Pennsylvania's law was *not* motivated by any effort to disenfranchise minorities or

Democratic voters—despite comments from a couple of GOP state legislators predicting that the law, if it stood, would reduce voter fraud in the overwhelmingly Democratic stronghold of Philadelphia.

What won't be helpful in the defense of voter-ID laws in other states was Judge McGinley's finding that the state offered no evidence to support its claim that the law was needed to block voter fraud. That decision by attorneys from the office of Kathleen Kane, the state's Democratic attorney general, badly undercuts supporters of the law.

It's not as if there aren't clues that voter fraud is a problem. In 2012, Philadelphia city commissioner Al Schmidt, a Republican, issued a 27-page report on irregularities he found in a sample of city precincts during that year's primary. The report, which looked at only 1 percent of the city's districts, found cases of double voting, voter impersonation, and voting by noncitizens, as well as 23 people who were not registered to vote but nonetheless voted. Schmidt also found reports of people who were counted as voting in the wrong party's primary. "We identified hundreds of cases of voting irregularities [in select precincts] that warrant further investigation," he concluded.

But his report was largely ignored by city officials, who operate in an environment that former Democratic governor Ed Rendell (and former Philadelphia mayor) admitted to me was "a yeasty system where the rule of law isn't always followed." Indeed, the city has long been a fount of corruption. This was also true when Republicans ran a machine that dominated the city for 80 years, until the 1950s; during that period, not a single Democrat was elected mayor, in part because of Republican-led voter fraud. All that changed after Democrats seized control of the levers of city power and bent them to their will.

Longtime observers of Philadelphia are quite candid about what goes on there. The late Arlen Specter, who served Pennsylvania in the U.S. Senate as both a Republican and a Democrat, openly scoffed at liberal claims that there was no voter fraud. "They don't see what they don't want to see," he told me in 2011. "I'm from Philadelphia. It's been a way of life here." Even after he became a Democrat, he stood by his 2007 GOP vote in favor of requiring photo IDs in all federal elections.

One reason for this is that Specter may once have been a victim of voter fraud himself. In 1967, he ran for mayor as a reform Republican against a Democratic machine that, Specter said, was "highly suspect if not demonstrably corrupt." Specter lost by 10,000 votes out of more than three-quarters of a million cast, and he strongly suspected that voter fraud played a big role in his loss.

Chris Matthews, the left-wing MSNBC host who hails from Pennsylvania, agrees that voter fraud is a Philly tradition. On *Hardball* he explained a common scheme there: Someone calls to enquire whether you voted or are going to vote, and "then all of a sudden, somebody does come and vote for you." Matthews says it's an old strategy in big-city politics: "I know all about it in North Philly—it's what went on, and I believe it still goes on."

Having said that, the same government entities that historically have failed to adequately address voter fraud also apparently botched the implementation of the state's voter-ID law. Judge McGinley found that the state deployed too few mobile units to issue voter IDs and that wait times at DMV offices for voter IDs were often long. The state also spent too little money on educating voters about the new law and often issued vague implementation regulations on the fly.

Any state looking to implement a sound voter-ID law must address these problems. Rhode Island secretary of state Ralph Mollis, a Democrat, convinced his state's left-leaning legislature to pass a photo-ID bill in 2011 to address problems of voter fraud in Providence and other cities. The law included extensive outreach efforts, with Mollis's office going to senior centers, homeless shelters, and community centers to process free IDs. The law has been implemented smoothly, Mollis says, and he views it as a national model.

Indeed, in 2005, a bipartisan Commission on Federal Election Reform, headed by former president Jimmy Carter and former secretary of state James Baker, issued 87 recommendations on how to clean up our system. One of its most important, support for national voter-ID, was based on the commission's finding that "the electoral system cannot inspire public confidence if no safeguards exist to deter or detect fraud or to confirm the identity of voters." Eighteen of the 21 commission members called for voters to show photo ID at the polls and for more security for absentee ballots.

Robert Pastor, the former executive director of the Carter-Baker commission (he also set up the Carter Center's election-monitoring programs), says he is disappointed that so few of the commission's recommendations have been implemented at the state or national level. In 2012, after a trip to Mexico, he compared that country's electoral system unfavorably with ours: "The Mexican electoral system is much fairer, professional, independent, and nonpartisan than the U.S. system." Every voter gets a biometric photo-ID card; the registration list is audited regularly; and the photos of the voters are on the list in each polling site.

Sadly, Pastor died this month, and his commonsense, bipartisan approach to making our election laws better will be missed. We need voter-ID laws to protect ballot integrity, and we also have to provide adequate resources to make sure voters have an ID. Such efforts should be in everyone's interests. Andrew Young, President Carter's U.N. ambassador, noted that, in an era when people have to show ID to travel, marry, or cash a check, "requiring ID can help poor people who otherwise might be even more marginalized by not having one."

When Pennsylvania's voter-ID law is either appealed or rewritten, let's hope that the state does a better job debunking the inflated estimates that hundreds of thousands of Pennsylvanians lacked an ID.

The state should also emphasize that even when voters show up at the polling place without an ID, they can vote on a provisional ballot. The state will count that ballot if the voter mails, faxes, or e-mails a copy of acceptable ID within six days of the election. If a person lacks the money to obtain the background documents necessary to acquire a voter ID, he can sign an affidavit attesting to that fact, after which his vote will be counted without further questions.

Pennsylvania officials should also explain that requiring voter IDs does more than keep fraudsters away from polling places. It also deters voting under false registrations and voting by illegal aliens and people registered in more than one state. U.S. Justice Department investigations in the past have shown that these types of fraud do take place in Pennsylvania.

As for allegations that there is scant evidence that people commit voter fraud at polling places, the Seventh Circuit Court of Appeals addressed these when it upheld Indiana's voter-ID law:

> There is voter fraud, specifically the form of voting fraud in which a person shows up at the polls claiming to be someone else—someone who has left the district, or died, too recently to have been removed from the list of registered voters, or someone who has not voted yet on election day. Without requiring a photo ID, there is little if any chance of preventing this kind of fraud because busy poll workers are unlikely to scrutinize signatures carefully and argue with people who deny having forged someone else's signature. . . . The absence of prosecutions is explained by the endemic under-enforcement of minor criminal laws (minor as they appear to the public and prosecutors, at all events) and by the extreme difficulty of apprehending a voter impersonator.

New York City's watchdog Department of Investigations proved how easy it is to commit in-person fraud last month when it issued a report detailing how its undercover agents showed up at 63 polling places and claimed to be individuals who had in fact died or moved out of town, or who were sitting in jail. In 61 instances, or 97 percent of the time, the testers were allowed to vote (they voted only for nonexistent write-in candidates). The city's Board of Elections, rather than examine its own sloppy procedures, responded by demanding that the investigators be prosecuted.

Pennsylvania's voter-ID law is in need of a tune-up, especially when it comes to outreach on free IDs. But the basic case for such laws hasn't been undermined by the decision of the Pennsylvania court. The vast majority of voters agree with the U.S. Supreme Court that properly drafted voter-ID laws are not overly burdensome. A 2012 *Washington Post* poll found that nearly two-thirds of African Americans and Hispanics back the requirement for photo IDs. And for good reason. Where strict voter-ID laws have been in operation for years, in states such as Indiana and Georgia, they have worked smoothly and the turnout of minority voters has in fact increased. Indeed, the Census Bureau has found that the rate of voter turnout for blacks exceeded that of whites for the first time in the 2012 election.

"When the day is done, my job is to maintain the integrity of elections," Mollis says in explaining his support for voter-ID in Rhode Island as well as in other states. "Even if a state doesn't have an immediate problem with fraud, doesn't it make sense to take sensible precautions rather than wait for someone to abuse the system, and then it's too late?"

> *"A spokeswoman for the Texas secretary of state's office . . . said she was not aware of anyone with a substantially similar name on their ID and voter registration being prevented from voting."*

Texas Is Not Restricting Women's Right to Vote

PolitiFact

PolitiFact is a project of the Tampa Bay Times *that is devoted to evaluating the truth of political statements. In the following viewpoint, the author notes that Democrats have claimed that the Texas voter identification (ID) law is intended to prevent women, who change their names more often than men, from voting for Democratic gubernatorial candidate Wendy Davis. The author says that there is no evidence that the law, first proposed in 2011, was intended to affect Wendy Davis's campaign in 2014. Moreover, there is no clear evidence that the law will disenfranchise women, since women who have similar names to their ID can simply swear the ID is accurate and cast their vote. PolitiFact concludes that Democratic claims are inaccurate.*

As you read, consider the following questions:

1. According to the viewpoint, what exactly did the e-mail blast from the Democratic Governors Association say about the new voter ID law?

2. What concerns about the voter ID law did Wendy Davis express in 2011?

3. According to the author, at what point will there be evidence to evaluate the effect of the new voter ID law?

An Oct. 24, 2013, email blast from the Democratic Governors Association opened: "BREAKING: Texas Governor Rick Perry's voter ID law is a blatant effort to defeat [Democratic gubernatorial candidate] Wendy Davis by disenfranchising tens of thousands of women voters."

The email, urging donations to Davis's gubernatorial campaign, went on to say that Perry and "his handpicked successor, Greg Abbott," the Republican Texas attorney general running for governor, "are trying to undo the voting rights women fought for—a century ago! It's downright anti-democratic."

Dramatic—and is this so?

Time Line Wrong

From the top, there's a sizable time line hiccup in the idea that the Texas voter ID law, approved by the Republican-led legislature and signed into law by Perry in 2011, came to be in order to disenfranchise women potentially voting for Davis for governor in 2014. Davis, a Fort Worth state senator, announced her gubernatorial candidacy on Oct. 3, 2013, and wasn't even reported to be considering a statewide bid until after her June 25, 2013, filibuster slowing GOP-led passage of a measure stepping up abortion restrictions.

To our request for backup information, an association spokesman, Danny Kanner, emailed us links to a news article and commentary, both published in October 2013, and to a

2006 report by the Brennan Center for Justice at New York University. The articles touched on the possibility that photo IDs presented by women at the polls might not have the same names on them as voter records. None reached conclusions about a link between the 2011 law and Davis garnering votes for governor in 2014.

Under the Texas law, which had its implementation delayed to the November 2013 elections by legal challenges, voters going to the polls are expected to present a photo ID issued by the Texas Department of Public Safety (a driver's license, personal ID card, concealed handgun license or election identification certificate) or by the federal government (a passport, military ID or a citizenship or naturalization certificate).

As noted by Kanner, on Oct. 22, 2013, KIII-TV, Channel 3 in Corpus Christi, reported that the law may cause delays at polling places when a voter's name on their offered ID doesn't match their name on the voter roll. The story quoted a state district judge, Sandra Watts, as saying that when she went to vote the day before, what "I have used for voter registration and for identification for the last 52 years was not sufficient." Watts was required to sign an affidavit affirming her identity, the story said, when a poll official noticed that she had one name shown as her middle name on her driver's license and a different middle name on her voter registration card. One of the middle names was her maiden name.

The story further noted that the alternative to signing a voter affidavit would be to vote a provisional ballot. A provisional ballot isn't counted until seven to 10 days after an election and then only after a voter proves their eligibility.

On Oct. 24, 2013, *Slate* legal columnist Dahlia Lithwick wrote a commentary, also noted by Kanner, about the effect of voter ID laws on turnout. She concluded there is insufficient data to reach sweeping conclusions about the effects of voter ID laws on disenfranchising women. Lithwick noted first that some see an effort to deter females aligned with Democratic candidates from casting ballots. To the contrary, Lithwick wrote, some election law experts told her such laws might deter more conservative women who might be more likely to have different names on their voter registrations and photo IDs.

Kanner also pointed out a 2006 survey conducted by the Brennan Center indicating that only 48 percent of voting-age women with ready access to their birth certificates had a certificate with their current legal name. "Many of those who possess ready documentation of their citizenship do not have documentation that reflects their current name. For example, survey results show that only 48% of voting-age women with ready access to their U.S. birth certificates have a birth certificate with current legal name—and only 66% of voting-age women with ready access to any proof of citizenship have a document with current legal name. Using 2000 census citizen voting-age population data, this means that as many as 32 million voting-age women may have available only proof of citizenship documents that do not reflect their current name."

Concern about women being blocked from voting is one thing. We looked for signs the law was written to do so, coming up empty.

A Press Release and a News Blog Post

On the Nexis database, we searched for news articles on the 2011 Texas law and the disenfranchisement of women.

Many stories touched on Democratic charges that ID demands at the polls would deter Latino and black voters. Very little turned up focusing on the effects of the mandate on women.

On March 24, 2011, blogger Charles Kuffner of Houston quoted a press release issued by Houston state [representative] Jessica Farrar, a Democrat who opposed the proposal. Issued after the House advanced the ID measure, Farrar's release said: "The list of citizens who could be denied the right to vote because of the new requirement is quite lengthy, and includes the elderly, women who are recently married or divorced, college students, the poor, those who live in rural areas, Hispanics and African Americans."

Earlier, the *Fort Worth Star-Telegram* reported on Davis questioning the Senate's version of the ID measure by recalling her younger years while stressing the possible effect of the law on low-income Texans.

"Long before she was a Harvard-educated attorney and a member of the state Senate, Wendy Davis was a divorced single mom who was holding down two jobs and raising a young daughter while attending Tarrant County community college," the newspaper's Dave Montgomery said in a Jan. 25, 2011, *PoliTex* blog post. "Davis recalled those experiences Tuesday as the Republican-controlled state Senate debated a controversial voter ID bill. Like other Democrats, she contended that (Senate Bill) 14 threatens to disenfranchise the indigent, minorities and elderly by requiring voters to show a photo identification in order to vote," the post went.

The blog post continued: "'There was a time when I was indigent,' the Fort Worth lawmaker told Sen. Troy Fraser, R-Horseshoe Bay, as they debated the merits of the legislation. Had the law been in effect during her earlier days, Davis told Fraser, she 'would have been quite challenged' in acquiring the documentation needed to exercise her right to vote."

Davis cited her own experiences when she was holding down two jobs and said that many low-income Texans do not have the time to leave work and stand in long lines, nor do they have the money to purchase the required ID documents, Montgomery wrote. "For people who have to take off at work it can be a very real problem," Davis said as she stood beside a chart illustrating the cost of supporting documents, the blog post said. "I'm afraid we're going to wind up disenfranchising legal citizens . . . who are going to be denied the right to vote."

**Gender Gap in Voting for President,
Final Preelection Polls**

Year	Men	Women	Difference
2012	–8	+12	20 pts.
2008	0	+14	14 pts.
2004	–12	+4	16 pts.
2000	–7	+8	15 pts.
1996	+1	+15	14 pts.
1992	+4	+8	4 pts.
1988	–12	–4	8 pts.
1984	–28	–10	18 pts.
1980	–15	–5	10 pts.
1976	+8	–3	11 pts.
1972	–26	–24	2 pts.
1968	–2	+2	4 pts.
1964	+20	+24	4 pts.
1960	+4	–2	6 pts.
1956	–10	–22	12 pts.
1952	–6	–16	10 pts.

Figures represent lead/deficit for Democratic candidate among men and women in each election, in percentage points.

TAKEN FROM: Jeffrey M. Jones, "Gender Gap in 2012 Vote Is Largest in Gallup's History," Gallup, November 9, 2012.

More Women Might Lack
Required ID to Vote

Separately, we asked activists and attorneys who have questioned the law about evidence bearing on the association's claim.

Wendy Weiser, who directs a Brennan Center project focused on voting rights and who also has been involved in litigation against the law, said by telephone that she is not aware of studies specific to the ID mandate's effect on women alone, though she said that due to marriages and divorces, women generally change their names more often than men.

Weiser suggested we consider research by Matt Barreto, a University of Washington political scientist who has conducted voter surveys to gauge how many have the IDs required to vote in states with such mandates. By email, Barreto told us that a 2009 survey of Texas registered voters indicates that at that time, 89.5 percent of male registered voters had a valid photo ID compared with 84.2 percent of women. The difference, Barreto said, was statistically significant and an indication that about 900,000 registered female voters lacked the ID likely required to vote compared with about 520,000 men.

Arianna Campos, a Farrar aide, suggested we contact Sondra Haltom, president of Empower the Vote Texas, a nonprofit group that describes itself as advocating changes that encourage voter participation and opposing restrictions of voter rights. By telephone, Haltom said that by her analysis, a match of state voter rolls with driver license data, as of August 2013, nearly 610,000 registered voters had no sign of a driver's license or state ID on their voter registration records—with 84 percent of them being women and/or minorities and/or young people. Haltom emailed us a spreadsheet indicating that by her calculation, about 402,000 of the nearly 610,000 voters, 60 percent, were women.

But the state of Texas and federal judges have objected to reaching conclusions about how many people carry appropriate IDs based on such absences of matching information, a spokesman for Abbott's state office, Jerry Strickland, pointed out by email.

In August 2012, a judicial panel for the U.S. District Court for the District of Columbia issued a ruling striking down the Texas ID law, though that ruling was overtaken on June 25, 2013, when the Supreme Court held that Texas and other jurisdictions no longer had to win federal preclearance of changes in voting laws before carrying them out.

Regardless, the 2012 ruling said the state had failed to prove the ID law would not lead to retrogression in voting among racial minorities. That ruling also challenged the methodology behind tabulating those registration records lacking driver's license numbers. The judges noted, first, that Texans seeking to register to vote are given the option of recording the last four digits of a Social Security number or their eight-digit driver's license number, meaning "even voters who possess a driver's license may opt to provide a Social Security number. After all, four digits are easier to write than eight. Furthermore, many voters likely memorize their Social Security number but not their driver's license number," the judges wrote. "Thus, what voters write on their registration form is barely probative of whether they actually possess a state-issued ID card—much less whether they possess any" of the types of photo IDs permitted under the law.

State: No Voters Turned Away to Date

Finally, a spokeswoman for the Texas secretary of state's office, Alicia Pierce, telephoned us after learning of this fact check from the attorney general's office. Pierce stressed that the Texas law does not require anyone's name on a valid ID to perfectly match their name on their voter registration. She said, too, that voters whose names are "substantially" similar had cast ballots in the 2013 "early voting" period by swearing that they are who they say they are. Men and women were affected to limited degrees, she said. She said she was not aware of anyone with a substantially similar name on their ID and voter registration being prevented from voting.

The Democratic governors group said the voter ID measure signed into law by Perry is a "blatant effort to defeat Wendy Davis by disenfranchising tens of thousands of women voters."

In addition to its time line gulf—the ID proposal passed into law two years before Davis emerged as a serious gubernatorial prospect—this claim suffers from an absence of proof that the Texas law was intended to disenfranchise tens of thousands of women or has had such an immediate effect.

Significantly, we are not judging here whether the ID hurdle is affecting voter participation. The law is lately being enforced for the first time. Only after the 2013 elections is there likely to be data on its effect on voters—of all kinds.

This preelection claim, weakened by chronological illogic and an overall absence of evidence, shakes out as both incorrect and ridiculous. Pants on Fire!

Periodical and Internet Sources Bibliography

The following articles have been selected to supplement the diverse views presented in this chapter.

Jackie Calmes — "Obama Reassures Leaders on Enforcing Voting Rights," *New York Times*, July 29, 2013.

Wade Goodwyn — "Texas' Voter ID Law Creates a Problem for Some Women," NPR, October 30, 2013.

Richard L. Hasen — "Voter Suppression's New Pretext," *New York Times*, November 15, 2013.

Albert R. Hunt — "The Battle to Protect Voting Rights," *New York Times*, May 5, 2014.

Carrie Johnson — "Justice Department Sues North Carolina over Voter ID Law," NPR, September 30, 2013.

Karen Langley — "Pennsylvania Judge Strikes Down State's Voter ID Law," *Pittsburgh Post-Gazette*, January 17, 2014.

Dana Liebelson — "Voter ID Laws in Action: 'Looks Like I Don't Get to Vote Today,'" *Mother Jones*, November 6, 2013.

Bryan Preston — "Texas Voter ID Law Didn't Suppress Vote," CNN, November 12, 2013.

Maya Rhodan — "What the Voter ID Law Really Means for Women in Texas," *Time*, October 24, 2013.

Zachary Roth — "Pennsylvania Governor Won't Challenge Ruling Striking Down Voter ID Law," MSNBC, May 8, 2014.

Justin Udo — "Opponents of Pa. Voter ID Law Rejoice Gov. Corbett Will Not Appeal Decision," CBS Philly, May 8, 2014.

OPPOSING
VIEWPOINTS®
SERIES

CHAPTER 3

How Do Voting Rights Apply to Particular Groups?

Chapter Preface

In most jurisdictions in the United States, undocumented immigrants—those people in the country without proper papers—are not allowed to vote. However, in some locations they can vote, and some commenters argue that these voting rights should be expanded.

One major jurisdiction that has started to think about allowing undocumented immigrants to vote is New York City. The city council is considering a bill that allows undocumented immigrants to cast ballots if they have lived in the city for six months and passed all other requirements for voting. According to city council member Daniel Dromm, who coauthored the bill, "This is extremely important, because it's based on the founding principle of this country and that was, 'No Taxation Without Representation.' All of the people who would be included in this and would be allowed to vote are paying taxes, they've contributed to society," as quoted by Hunter Walker in a May 9, 2013, article at Talking Points Memo.

Other jurisdictions have not gone so far as to allow noncitizens to vote but have nonetheless taken steps to allow them greater participation in elections. California, for example, has moved to allow "noncitizens to sit on juries and monitor polls for elections," according to Jennifer Medina in a September 20, 2013, article in the *New York Times*.

Some commenters have objected strongly to the suggestion that noncitizens be allowed to vote. For example, L. Vincent Poupard in a December 15, 2011, post at Yahoo News objects to a proposal by New Haven mayor John DeStefano to grant the right to vote to undocumented immigrants. Poupard argues that "the thought of granting voting rights to people who are here illegally is a slap in the face to every American citizen. The idea is a slap in the face to anyone who entered this country legally and has gone through the steps to become a citizen." Poupard suggests that DeStefano's move was partisan and an effort by Democrats to enlist new voters who would probably tend to support them in elections.

Along the same lines, Stanley A. Renshon in a September 2008 report for the Center for Immigration Studies argues that the citizenship process is an important part of becoming an American and learning what it means to be an American. Thus, he says:

> You cannot really learn about America without living here. You cannot understand or take part in America without understanding its language. And you cannot begin to form the more enduring attachments to the national community that you have asked to join without first taking an affirmative step in that direction. For all these reasons, naturalization as a requirement of citizenship and voting is not so much a series of hurdles to surmount, but an essential part of becoming American.

The following chapter examines the voting rights of particular groups in America, including legal immigrants, children, felons, and mentally disabled individuals.

> "Unquestionably, immigrants will com-
> pose a greater share of the population
> in the years to come. If the United
> States is to be a truly inclusive democ-
> racy, we must ensure they have every
> opportunity to participate in the policy-
> making process by voting."

Encouraging Immigrants to Vote Strengthens Democracy

Tova Andrea Wang

Tova Andrea Wang is a senior fellow at Demos and an expert on election reform and political participation in the United States and internationally. She is the author of The Politics of Voter Suppression: Defending and Expanding Americans' Right to Vote. *In the following viewpoint, she argues that immigrants can play an important role in elections and that political parties and candidates should focus on increasing the participation of immigrant groups in voting. She points to the success of Barack Obama's election outreach effort to Hispanic and Asian communities, and she says candidates with immigrant backgrounds have also been shown to mobilize ethnic communities. She says that organizational efforts and government support for registering and involving immigrants could substantially increase voter participation among ethnic populations.*

As you read, consider the following questions:

1. What statistics does Wang provide to show historically low levels of voting by immigrants?

2. What examples does Wang list of instances in which immigrant candidates increased immigrant turnout?

3. How does language have an impact on voting, according to Wang?

As was vividly demonstrated in the 2012 election, immigrant communities are increasingly a major political and civic force. A record 10 percent of the electorate in 2012 was Latino, up a percentage point from 2008, and the Asian-American share of the electorate rose to 3 percent, still small but historic. Both groups overwhelmingly voted for President [Barack] Obama, in even larger proportions than they did in 2008, proving themselves to be potent voting blocs.

Growing Influence

They are poised to become even more influential in the near future. The Pew Hispanic Center reports that Hispanics will account for 40 percent of the growth in the electorate over the next two decades. By 2030, 40 million Hispanics will be eligible voters, up from 23.7 million today. If Hispanics' voter participation and naturalization rates increase to the levels of other groups, the number of Hispanic votes cast could double within two decades. Similarly, the Asian share of the electorate is estimated to more than double by 2040.

Nonetheless, even as the trends show growth, voting by naturalized citizens overall (as opposed to voters from immigrant backgrounds generally) still lags. While we do not have exact numbers for the 2012 election, the data from recent years are telling. In 2008, turnout among the native-born voting-age population was 64.4 percent and only 54 percent among naturalized voting-age Americans. The disparity in turnout between native and naturalized Americans has been persistent; in 2006, naturalized citizens voted at a rate 12 percentage points lower than their native counterparts—49 percent versus 37 percent—and in 2004, there was an 11-point gap.

Further, although voting is extremely important, it is not the only measure of political and civic participation. Studies indicate a gap in other forms of civic engagement as well, including volunteering for an organization, contacting a government official, signing a petition, and working for or donating to a political campaign.

So what can be done?

Voter Registration and Voting

Historically the parties have not seen it in their interest to invest in the naturalized-citizen population because it does not fit within their "win now" mentality. Parties and candidates have focused their energies on people who are already registered and likely to vote, a smaller and easier-to-target slice of the population—and one that has usually not included immigrants. Party and candidate outreach to Latinos has been growing as their population has grown, but it remains limited for the most part, oftentimes amounting to generic Spanish-language ads. Outreach to other communities, including the Asian population, has been even more wanting.

However, the Obama campaign broke from that history, beginning in 2008 and in a more significant way in 2012. Given demographers' prediction of the exponential growth in the Latino and Asian populations, it's easy to see how the Democrats' efforts in 2012 are only the beginning of a shift toward mobilizing these groups, especially given their growing propensity to vote Democratic. Both ethnic groups are now realizing how critically important they can be in shifting election outcomes when operating more or less as a bloc.

Just after his inauguration in 2009, the Obama administration reached out to Latinos directly through Spanish-language media, including media that had never before had access to the White House. Then, in 2011, the Obama campaign launched a ground game—door-to-door efforts, information sessions, tables at community events—to register Latinos, especially youth. This was exciting to see: a political campaign seeking to register *new* voters, adding more people to the electorate, rather than just relying on turning out return customers.

In heavily Asian areas, there was greater party turnout than ever before. According to a report from a coalition of Asian-American organizations, "Unlike previous election cycles, where the Asian American vote was viewed as marginal to presidential campaigns, 2012 saw attention and some strategic efforts by the parties to focus on Asian American voters in Nevada, Virginia, Pennsylvania, and Ohio."

But it was still not nearly sufficient. Even though there were improvements in 2012, the report notes:

> One of the key stories about Asian American voters for 2012 was the lack of investment in outreach to this ever-growing electorate. Preelection surveys found that Asian Americans had minimal contact by candidates, parties, or other groups and that about 2 in 3 Asian American likely voters were not contacted about the upcoming election. Considering that almost a third of the community was still undecided a month prior to Election Day, parties and other organizations missed an important opportunity to educate Asian American voters and potentially build future bases of support.

Candidates and Officials Matter

Candidates also have a role to play. When it comes to the naturalized-citizen vote, candidates—and what they believe, do, and say—matter. If the community doesn't like the candidates or their positions, or feel alienated by the candidate's lack of attention to the community and its interests, even strong mobilization efforts will make only a marginal difference. Like any other constituency, immigrant voters need a reason to turn out to vote beyond just a sense of civic duty. A few ads in Spanish won't suffice. As much as with other groups, candidates must speak to issues in ways that attract immigrant citizens. And as with other groups, candidates must *want* the votes of these Americans and make that clear.

Government officials also must do their part. In some areas of the country, election officials take a proactive approach to registering new Americans. In most parts of the country, they do not. This needs to change, including in places where minority-language assistance is not required under the law. At a minimum, it is neither expensive nor labor intensive to make voter-registration forms in alternative languages widely available, and to provide voter assistance in those languages as well through a hotline. The Election Assistance Commission, the federal agency that provides guidance on election practices in the United States, has commendably provided voting materials and registration forms in several languages and posted them on its website. Some jurisdictions—Minnesota and Cook County, Illinois come to mind—do an excellent job of providing such materials now, but other state and local government officials can easily make better use of this service.

Moreover, the U.S. Citizenship and Immigration Services, which is responsible for naturalization ceremonies, has recently issued formal guidance requiring voter registration at all naturalization ceremonies throughout the country by either election officials, nonprofit organizations, or, if necessary, agency officials themselves. This guidance must be fully implemented and monitored for compliance. By simply registering new citizens, we could see hundreds of thousands of new voters every year.

Recent research tells us that another way to increase immigrant turnout is to have more immigrant candidates. Matt Barreto, a political scientist at the University of Washington, has written extensively about the mobilizing impact a "co-ethnic" candidate can have on immigrant communities. In a study of five mayoral races across the country, Barreto found that having a Latino candidate led to significantly higher turnout for that candidate regardless of party or country of origin. And there are strong indications this is not just a phenomenon limited to Latino candidates, as demonstrated by former Minnesota state senator Mee Moua's experience turning out the Hmong-American community in St. Paul and U.S. Representative Judy Chu's ability to turn out Asian-American voters in California. These are encouraging trends. According to a report by the New American Leaders Project (NALP), there were 80 congressional candidates from immigrant communities in 2012: 55 Latinos, 17 Asian Americans, six Arab Americans, and two Caribbean Americans. Forty-seven won. Tulsi Gabbard is the first American Samoan in Congress, Mazie Hirono is the first Asian-American woman in the U.S. Senate, and now there are a dozen Asian Americans in Congress.

If candidates with immigrant backgrounds have the ability to inspire their communities to get more involved, we need to cultivate and support more immigrants to run for office. As I discuss below, community organizations and labor unions can serve as "incubators" for immigrant activists, teaching them leadership and organizing skills. One of the most encouraging projects in this regard is NALP. Among other activities, the project recruits promising leaders from immigrant communities and invites them to participate in a two-day training program called "Ready to Lead," which emphasizes the immigrant experience as a campaign asset. After the session, participants are coached by webinar to prepare for advanced campaign skills training. These types of innovations need to be supported to grow and reach all corners of the country.

Voting-Eligible Population, Actual and Projected: 2012 and 2030 (in millions)

Population	2012	2030	Share of growth
All	215	256	100%
Hispanic	24	40	40%
White	154	163	23%
Black	27	35	21%
Asian	9	16	15%

Notes: "White," "Black," and "Asian" include only the non-Hispanic components of those populations. American Indian/Alaska Native not shown. "Share" calculated before rounding.

Source: Pew Hispanic Center tabulations of the August 2012 Current Population Survey and Pew Research Center projections, 2012.

TAKEN FROM: Jon Perr, "GOP Still Fixates on Border Security as Illegal Immigration Plummets," *Daily Kos*, June 20, 2013.

Bolstering Civic Engagement

Engaging immigrants in civic activity beyond voting is also critical to the health of our democracy. There are many ways to make one's voice heard.

Community organizations, including social service and advocacy groups, are the primary mobilizers of immigrant communities toward all forms of political engagement. As scholar Janelle Wong has written, community-based mobilization creates the foundation for mass mobilization by teaching immigrants communication and organizing skills, and giving them the confidence to participate. Such organizations are particularly effective at reaching people who are seen as the most difficult to engage: people with few resources, those who may not speak English as a first language, and even noncitizens. As another scholar, Els de Graauw, has written, immigrant organizations serve as "civic incubators" and provide participants with opportunities to develop leadership potential and skills such as budgeting, personnel practices, and bargaining.

Many organizations didn't claim victory on Election Day and leave it at that, but pivoted toward issue-based advocacy. In December [2012], a coalition of Latino advocacy groups announced a civic engagement campaign to pass comprehensive immigration reform. This is a hopeful sign that the normal pattern can be reversed: Immigrants can be mobilized first to vote, and then encouraged to engage in other forms of political and civic activity.

Scholars of civic participation have increasingly recognized the critical role unions play in mobilizing immigrant engagement. As immigrants have become vital to union membership, it's been found that union participation contributes to the political incorporation of Latino immigrants. One recent study discovered that parents who were in unions used the civic engagement and advocacy skills learned through union activity to organize for improvements at their children's schools. Examining immigrants in one particular union, the researchers found that it served as a "'school for democracy' by granting parent members with the confidence, skills, and experience useful for political engagement in their children's schools." De Graauw has called unions essential to immigrant civic engagement, and has explored numerous examples of unions taking immigrant members from workplace mobilization to other forms of civic participation across the country.

Finally, civic and language education is essential to engaging immigrants. Many studies show that length of time in the country is key to whether a naturalized citizen will participate politically. These studies suggest that as an immigrant becomes more familiar with American politics and culture and feels a greater sense of belonging to this country, she becomes more inclined to participate. But this shouldn't take the 20 years academics find it currently takes to accomplish. Increased resources and interest in providing civic education, civic skill-building, and systems through which immigrants learn about and participate in our democracy even prior to attaining citizenship would go a long way in reducing the time it takes a naturalized citizen to become inclined to register to vote.

Providing resources for immigrants to learn English is a major part of this. We know that language has a direct impact on voter participation, and on civic, economic, and social integration in general. Recent legislative efforts at immigration reform will demand even greater levels of proficiency in English than ever before. Yet the government provides only a small fraction of the resources necessary to allow new Americans and other immigrants to learn English. This includes the public schools. If we want to close the participation gap between native-born and naturalized citizens in our system of governance, this must change. As the Migration Policy Institute has documented at length, the gap between those who need English-language instruction and the number of classes available is enormous. The institute has proposed concrete ways to pay for such instruction and has demonstrated what a solid return on investment such spending would provide.

Unquestionably, immigrants will compose a greater share of the population in the years to come. If the United States is to be a truly inclusive democracy, we must ensure they have every opportunity to participate in the policy-making process by voting and engaging in the entirety of civic and communal activities. Immigrants themselves are clearly taking the lead, and with improvements to our political structure and civic infrastructure they will flourish and contribute to the well-being of all Americans.

> *"While the liberal media and the liberal establishment ignore what is a huge scandal, American voters are having their rights violated."*

Fraudulent Voting by Illegal Immigrants Is a Serious Problem

Jim Kouri

Jim Kouri is vice president of the National Association of Chiefs of Police; he writes a column for the RenewAmerica website and contributes articles to many police and security magazines. In the following viewpoint, he argues that illegal immigrants are voting fraudulently in American elections. He says that Democrats encourage such fraud because most immigrants vote for Democratic candidates. He says that the 2000 presidential election, which Republican George W. Bush won, may have been more decisive if not for the votes of illegal immigrants, and he suggests that other election results have been altered as well. He concludes that more needs to be done to protect the integrity of the American vote.

As you read, consider the following questions:

1. According to Kouri, what prevents President Obama from discussing investigations of ACORN?

2. How do some states verify that voters are citizens, according to Kouri?

3. What election result in Minnesota does Kouri suggest may have been affected by illegal voting?

While the mainstream news media are beginning to cover the story of rampant voter fraud perpetrated by liberal organizations such as ACORN [Association of Community Organizations for Reform Now], don't expect reporters to provide any more than a passing interest in preventing illegal aliens—or even legal immigrants—from voting.

Democrats and Fraud

While President Barack Obama scolded corporate America, his service as an attorney for ACORN in the past prevents him from even once mentioning local, state and federal investigations of that organization as a result of numerous voter fraud allegations.

When voters discover fraud by a candidate, they react. For example, in a 2006 congressional race in Southern California between Republican Brian Bilbray and Democrat Francine Busby, Busby told a room full of illegal aliens that they didn't need "papers"—meaning identification—to vote. Thank goodness it was recorded and played on talk radio shows across the nation. Busby lost because she got caught saying what many other Democrats may tell illegal aliens.

A recent study released by the conservative think tank the Heritage Foundation provides proof that illegal aliens and immigrants with green cards are committing rampant voter fraud in the United States.

Reports of ineligible persons registering to vote have raised concerns about state processes for verifying voter registration lists. States usually base voter eligibility on the voter's age, US citizenship, mental competence, and felon status.

Although individual states run elections, Congress has authority to affect the administration of the elections. The Help America Vote Act of 2002 (HAVA) had set a deadline for states to have a statewide voter registration list and list verification procedures.

For example, the methods used in seven selected states to verify voter eligibility and ensure accuracy of voter registration lists were varied and include relying on registrant self-attestation, return mailings, and checking against lists of felony convictions or deceased individuals. Some states, for instance, failed to do any more than ask on their application forms if the registrant was a US citizen. The applicant will merely check off the "Yes" box, but there is no action taken to verify the authenticity of that answer.

"The voter registration officials simply take the word of the registrant with no follow-up," said conservative political strategist Michael Baker.

"Some states that require some backup documentation merely ask for a utility bill or a driver's license—neither of which prove citizenship. In other words, legal or illegal aliens can easily register to vote in local and national elections," warns Baker.

According to a congressional study of voter fraud, other challenges such as identifying duplicate registrations in other states or having insufficient information to match other data sources with voter registration lists may continue to be issues.

While federal data sources have the potential to help state election officials identify registrants who may be convicted felons or noncitizens, few states communicate with federal agencies such as the Homeland Security Department's immigration section.

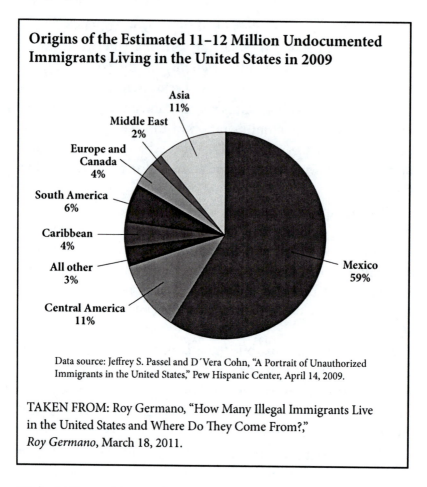

Origins of the Estimated 11–12 Million Undocumented Immigrants Living in the United States in 2009

Asia
11%

Middle East
2%

Europe and
Canada
4%

South America
6%

Caribbean
4%

All other
3%

Central America
11%

Mexico
59%

Data source: Jeffrey S. Passel and D'Vera Cohn, "A Portrait of Unauthorized Immigrants in the United States," Pew Hispanic Center, April 14, 2009.

TAKEN FROM: Roy Germano, "How Many Illegal Immigrants Live in the United States and Where Do They Come From?," *Roy Germano*, March 18, 2011.

Illegal Votes in 2000

Many government officials—mostly liberals—claim that illegal aliens' voting is not a major problem; conservative activists respond that while the potential number identified may be small, an election can be decided by a few votes. In 2000, the presidential race between Democrat Al Gore and Republican George W. Bush was decided by a few hundred votes in Florida.

"While the news media perpetuated the assertion that Bush and the GOP 'stole' the election, it could very well have been illegal aliens voting in Florida that made the outcome so close," said former NYPD [New York City Police Department] cop, now security firm owner, Sid Francis.

"Bush may have beaten Gore by more votes if illegals were excluded, since immigrants tend to vote for Democrats. Or Gore could have won decisively had there been prior screening before people were allowed into the voting booths," said Det. Francis.

"There was absolutely no mention in the mainstream media regarding suspected voter fraud by illegal or legal aliens. It was much easier for the agenda-driven newspeople to accuse Republicans of stealing the election," added Baker.

"Florida is not unique. Thousands of noncitizens are registered to vote in some states, and tens if not hundreds of thousands in total may be present on the voter rolls nationwide. These numbers are significant: Local elections are often decided by only a handful of votes, and even national elections have likely been within the margin of the number of noncitizens illegally registered to vote," said Hans A. von Spakovsky, a researcher at the Heritage Foundation.

"There is no reliable method to determine the number of noncitizens registered or actually voting because most laws to ensure that only citizens vote are ignored, are inadequate, or are systematically undermined by government officials. Those who ignore the implications of noncitizen registration and voting either are willfully blind to the problem or may actually favor this form of illegal voting," said Spakovsky, an expert on the subject of illegal aliens and immigration law, during an interview on Fox News Channel.

As far as felons, US attorneys are required to notify state election officials of federal felony convictions, but the information is not always easy for election officials to interpret or complete, according to New Jersey GOP strategist Janice Martin.

"Americans would be shocked to discover that hundreds of thousands of general election voters are illegal aliens, green-card immigrants, and criminals who've murdered, raped and robbed US citizens. And guess which political party benefits the most from their votes? The one that's pushing for amnesty and a bag full of free goodies," said Martin.

Spakovsky believes many government officials and politicians are complicit in the voter fraud problem.

"To keep noncitizens from diluting citizens' votes, immigration and election officials must cooperate far more effectively than they have to date, and state and federal officials must increase their efforts to enforce the laws against noncitizen voting that are already on the books," he wrote in his Heritage Foundation study on illegal alien voter fraud.

Canceling the Votes of Americans

Just last month [June 2009], in an extremely close race in Minnesota between incumbent senator Norm Coleman and comedian Al Franken, Franken was finally declared a winner months after the actual election. While the recount battle raged, no one within the government or within the news media gave a thought to investigating whether or not illegal aliens or legal immigrants voted in Minnesota for that contested senate seat. Franken's win gives the Democrats something they dreamed of achieving—a 60-seat majority that would ward off any Republican filibuster of their liberal-left legislation. "While the liberal media and the liberal establishment ignore what is a huge scandal, American voters are having their rights violated. When an illegal alien or felon or other person prohibited by law to vote [votes], their votes cancel out those of American citizens," warns Baker.

"Liberals want illegal aliens and felons to vote. They benefit from such rampant fraud."

> *"Contemporary voter ID laws are trying to solve a problem that hasn't existed in over a century."*

Voter Fraud Is Not a Serious Problem

Amy Bingham

Amy Bingham is a journalist for ABC News. In the following viewpoint, she reports that voter fraud almost never occurs in Texas and is even rarer in the rest of the United States. She interviews experts who point out that for immigrants and noncitizens, the benefit of voting illegally is far outweighed by the serious fines and possible deportation that can result for those caught casting illegal ballots. Opponents of voter identification (ID) laws say that such laws attempt to solve a problem that does not exist and may end up disenfranchising legal voters. Proponents of the law argue that having voters show an ID is common sense and a reasonable expectation.

As you read, consider the following questions:

1. Who is Reyna Almanza, and what did she do, according to Bingham?

2. How many cases of voter fraud does Bingham report occurred between 2002 and 2005?

3. According to the viewpoint, what sorts of punishment can someone who votes fraudulently face?

Reyna Almanza and her son strolled into the Progreso, Texas, school board election in 2009 just like 1,100 of their neighbors, cast their ballots and left. But hours later Almanza took her son back to the polls, where he used his incarcerated brother's name to vote a second time, breaking election laws and landing both mother and son in court.

Voter Impersonation

It is that kind of voter fraud that Texas's voter ID law, which was struck down in federal court last month [August 2012], and similar laws passed in eight states over the past two years were written to prevent. But voter impersonation cases like Almanza's, who is serving 5 years of probation for illegal voting, are the exception, not the norm.

Over the past decade, Texas has convicted 51 people of voter fraud, according the state's attorney general Greg Abbott. Only four of those cases were for voter impersonation, the only type of voter fraud that voter ID laws prevent.

Nationwide that rate of voter impersonation is even lower.

Out of the 197 million votes cast for federal candidates between 2002 and 2005, only 40 voters were indicted for voter fraud, according to a Department of Justice study outlined during a 2006 congressional hearing. Only 26 of those cases, or about .00000013 percent of the votes cast, resulted in convictions or guilty pleas.

But the push for voter ID laws is not all about preventing fraud, said Pennsylvania state representative Daryl Metcalfe, who sponsored his state's voter ID law.

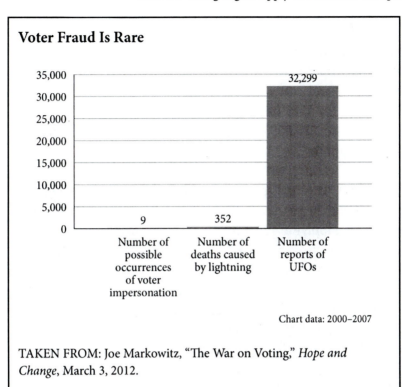

Voter Fraud Is Rare

Number of possible occurrences of voter impersonation: 9
Number of deaths caused by lightning: 352
Number of reports of UFOs: 32,299

Chart data: 2000–2007

TAKEN FROM: Joe Markowitz, "The War on Voting," *Hope and Change*, March 3, 2012.

"The driving factor is common sense," Metcalfe told ABC News. "It only makes sense that when you show up to vote, to exercise that very important right and responsibility, that you prove you are who you claim."

Metcalfe said the number of voter fraud cases that are prosecuted are only a sliver of the fraud taking place because there is no system in place to detect fraud. His voter ID law aims to do just that.

But opponents of the law claim that it is trying to solve a nonexistent problem.

"The point here is that people just don't do that," Lorraine Minnite, an associate professor of public policy at Rutgers University–Camden, said of committing voter fraud. "It just doesn't make sense."

Costs and Benefits

Minnite said there is little to no motivation for voters to attempt to impersonate someone else at the polls or for noncitizens to try and cast a ballot, a right reserved only for citizens. The price for that one vote is up to 5 years in prison and a fine of up to $10,000 for citizens and could mean deportation for immigrants.

That's exactly what happened to Usman Ali, a Pakistani immigrant who had lived in the United States as a permanent resident for 20 years. Ali checked the "yes" box to register to vote while applying for a driver's license in Florida.

Although he never tried to vote, Ali was deported back to Pakistan for allegedly committing voter fraud.

"What are the costs for noncitizens to cast ballots and what are the benefits? It doesn't add up," said Minnite, who testified against Pennsylvania's voter ID law. "The costs are very high and the benefits are practically nonexistent."

Tracy Campbell, a history professor at the University of Kentucky who studies voter fraud in past elections, said contemporary voter ID laws are trying to solve a problem that hasn't existed in over a century.

"This would prevent you from going to the polls and claiming that you're Mary Smith so you vote as Mary Smith then you come back later and vote as Mary Joan," Campbell said. "Repeating was a problem a century ago and these laws would have been good for that, but it's a non-event now."

In trying to solve that problem, critics say, the new voter ID laws could disenfranchise hundreds of thousands of voters who cannot obtain the necessary documents. In Pennsylvania, where Metcalfe's voter ID law will be in effect for the November election, at least 90,000 eligible voters did not have an ID that met the law's requirements to vote, according to initial estimates by the Pennsylvania Department of State.

But Metcalfe said he does not think the voter ID law will prevent people from going to the polls.

"With every right comes a responsibility," the Pennsylvania lawmaker said. "There is a responsibility now in Pennsylvania that goes along with being able to vote and that is when you show up on Election Day to have that photo ID."

> *"The restoration of voting rights to felons would not only contribute to a more robust democracy and the advancement of civil rights, but also would aid law enforcement and ensure fair and accurate voter rolls."*

Felons Should Be Enfranchised

Candice Bernd

Candice Bernd is an assistant editor and reporter with Truthout. In the following viewpoint, she reports on Attorney General Eric Holder's argument that disenfranchising felons, many of whom are black, is linked to the disenfranchisement of African Americans during the Jim Crow era. Bernd suggests that Holder may not be going far enough, since his stated opposition does little to lower the number of people incarcerated and has no effect on voting rules, which are established by the states. She notes that enfranchising felons would strengthen democracy and would make voting administration easier.

As you read, consider the following questions:

1. According to Bernd, how many states disenfranchise felons for life, and how do other states treat felons?

2. What concrete steps does Bruce A. Dixon say Holder could take if he was serious about changing laws around disenfranchisement of felons?

3. What is Rand Paul doing to address the disenfranchisement of felons, according to the viewpoint?

Attorney General Eric Holder this week [in February 2014] called on states to do away with arcane laws that prohibit more than 6 million felons, most of whom are people of color, from voting in a speech at Georgetown University Law Center.

Felons and Jim Crow

"Those swept up in this system too often had their rights rescinded, their dignity diminished, and the full measure of their citizenship revoked for the rest of their lives," Holder said in the speech. "They could not vote."

Currently, four states disenfranchise for life those convicted of felonies, and seven states permanently disenfranchise those with at least some kind of criminal convictions. Only two states, Maine and Vermont, allow those convicted of crimes to vote without restrictions.

Holder characterized these state policies as the remnants of the racist Jim Crow system in the South in the aftermath of the Civil War, in which states enacted laws to control and oppress people of color and to keep them from voting.

"It is important to remember that these laws disenfranchising people with criminal convictions have some of their roots in some of our country's most shameful past and serve to prevent communities of color from translating their numbers into a free and fair and accurate percentage of the voting population," said Myrna Pérez, deputy director of the democracy program at the Brennan Center for Justice. "It is an important recognition of the fact that goals of reintegration are not furthered by having people who cannot participate in our body politic."

According to a 2009 Brennan Center study, the restoration of voting rights to felons would not only contribute to a more robust democracy and the advancement of civil rights, but also would aid law enforcement and ensure fair and accurate voter rolls by relieving the administrative problems that accompany disenfranchisement polices.

"The act of voting is pregnant with so many good virtues that it totally stands to reason that people who engage in those good virtues are going to be people who are more successful when they are reintegrated," Pérez said.

But the states don't have to adhere to Holder's calls for change because state law sets the rules by which people can vote, which has caused the [Barack] Obama administration great consternation on other voting rights issues such as voter identification laws, which have been shown to prevent people of color and the poor from going to the polls. Holder, in August 2013, called for the elimination of mandatory minimum sentences for nonviolent drug offenders.

Since Holder's Tuesday speech, Republican leaders have indicated they are not willing to budge on their state policies, with Frank Collins, a spokesman for Florida governor Rick Scott, telling the *New York Times* that Holder's speech "has no effect on Florida's Constitution, which prescribes that individuals who commit felonies forfeit their right to vote."

More Efforts Needed

And the idea that Holder's speech is simply scratching at the surface of the issue to pay lip service to civil rights and mass incarceration without seriously addressing the problems certainly holds water for some. Bruce A. Dixon, managing editor of the *Black Agenda Report* who also serves on the state committee for the Georgia Green Party, said the speech was another indicator of what he called the black political establishment's complacency with issues of mass incarceration.

The History of Felon Disenfranchisement

In the United States, disenfranchisement of felons became common in the South (and in some northern states as well) following the Civil War. Disenfranchisement laws were designed primarily as "insurance" against recently enfranchised ex-slaves who might try to vote. But the list of crimes causing disenfranchisement was peculiar, to say the least. Mississippi included a provision in its 1890 state constitution for disenfranchising those convicted of burglary, theft, arson, and obtaining money under false pretenses, but not for robbery or murder. . . .

Currently, states differ substantially on the degree to which felons are allowed to vote, including those who are no longer in prison. The U.S. Constitution is silent on the question of felons' voting rights, thus allowing individual states to create whatever policies they please. Forty-eight states and the District of Columbia do not allow felons in prison to vote; Maine and Vermont do, along with the Commonwealth of Puerto Rico. Thirty-two states disenfranchise felons on parole; twenty-eight felons on probation. In fourteen states, felons are de facto disenfranchised for life because restoration of voting rights is an exceptionally onerous process, often requiring a gubernatorial pardon, clemency, complex and costly administrative appeals, or special acts of the state legislature (possibly with an extraordinary majority). In six of these states, restoration of voting rights is essentially impossible, while in the eight others it is extraordinarily difficult.

Richard K. Scher, The Politics of Disenfranchisement:
Why Is It So Hard to Vote in America?
New York: M.E. Sharpe, 2011.

"Their concern with the issue is like drive-by deep. If they can get away with making a few pronouncements, and keeping people on the hook so that they'll line up and vote for the Democrats again in the next year, then that's all they'll do," Dixon said. "They don't really have any skin in the game in any important way ... they're not trying to shrink the numbers of people in prison."

Dixon pointed to the track record of political officials, like Holder, who he says have done little to rein in organizations like the National Association of Assistant United States Attorneys, which has issued statements defending policies widely held to contribute to the mass incarceration of people of color.

"If Holder and his bosses really meant to do anything about mass incarceration they could make heads roll among these assistant US district attorneys, or they could engage in some public rhetoric against them to set the table for a national discussion of this stuff," Dixon said. "It's really not just Eric Holder; it's the entire black political class."

One sure route to enfranchise felons would be to pass the Democracy Restoration Act, cosponsored by Senator Benjamin Cardin (D-Md.) and Representative John Conyers (D-Mich.). The bill would restore the right to vote to American citizens who are released from prison or serving probation sentences, but the bill has languished since it was introduced in 2009.

Senator Rand Paul (R-Ky.) is drafting a somewhat similar bill, the Civil Rights Voting Restoration Act, for restoration of voting rights for those convicted of nonviolent felonies. Rand opposes disenfranchisement law in Kentucky, which is among the states barring voting rights from felons for life.

Dixon argued for an amendment to the Constitution that would guarantee the right to vote to all. "Once you make the right to vote a constitutional right, then that means no county court and no state government can make up laws that will impede it unless they fit federal guidelines. It also means that there will be uniform standards nationwide for how votes are counted and how elections are run."

> *"Suggesting that the automatic restoration of voting rights to all felons would lower recidivism is rather like suggesting that we can raise the incomes of all college students if we automatically grant them a college degree."*

What Holder Isn't Saying About Letting Felons Vote

Michael B. Mukasey

Michael B. Mukasey has served as US attorney general and as a US district judge. In the following viewpoint, he argues that allowing felons to be enfranchised would do little to reduce recidivism. He also argues that the Constitution explicitly allows states to disenfranchise people who commit serious crimes, and he suggests that this is justified as a way to show moral disapprobation of crimes. He argues that Democrats such as Attorney General Eric Holder support enfranchising felons because felons are disproportionately minorities and are likely to vote for Democrats. Mukasey dismisses the suggestion that the disenfranchisement of felons has anything to do with racial bias.

As you read, consider the following questions:

1. According to the viewpoint, what does Florida require of felons who want to regain their voting rights?

2. Which amendments does Mukasey say enshrine states' abilities to disenfranchise felons?

3. How do the states of Maine and Vermont treat felon enfranchisement, according to Mukasey?

There is a worthwhile debate to be had over whether state laws that disenfranchise felons should be changed or even eliminated. There can be an interesting discussion of how the history of such laws affects that debate. But you would not have known that from Eric Holder's treatment of the subject in a Feb. 10 [2014] speech at the Georgetown [University] Law Center in Washington.

The U.S. attorney general told us that statistics can be read to show that felon disenfranchisement laws actually promote recidivism. He said that such laws, which vary from state to state, are rooted in outdated notions going back to colonial days (when no one did any voting). He said that they were used during Reconstruction intentionally, and have been used since (whether intentionally or not is left hanging in the air) to deny the vote to blacks—who make up a larger percentage of those convicted of felonies than they do of the general population.

The statistical argument derives from a recent study in Florida that showed a lower recidivism rate for felons whose right to vote had been restored than for those whose right hadn't. However, there is more going on here.

Florida has had, and indeed has broadened, a system that requires felons to go through an application process before their voting rights are restored. Obviously, those who are motivated to navigate such a process self-select as a group less likely to repeat their crimes. Suggesting that the automatic restoration of voting rights to all felons would lower recidivism is rather like suggesting that we can raise the incomes of all college students if we automatically grant them a college degree—because statistics show that people with college degrees have higher incomes than those without them.

The history suggested by the attorney general is just as deeply flawed. A clue to the flaw lies in his failure to call for a federal law barring state felon disenfranchisement statutes. Why would an administration given to bold legislative action at the federal level—given to bold action even *without* legislation—shrink from calling for such action here?

The omission becomes less curious when one considers that the history of felon disenfranchisement statutes is tied up intimately in constitutional history. Most particularly, it is tied up with the history of what are known as the Reconstruction amendments: the 13th, 14th and 15th Amendments to the Constitution—the very amendments that ended slavery and set out the basic guarantees of equality for all under state law.

Abolitionists, viewed at the time as radicals, embraced what has been called a philosophy of formal equality. They not only insisted on the liberation and enfranchisement of former slaves, but also supported the disenfranchisement of criminals, rebels and other wrongdoers.

In its first section, the 14th Amendment guarantees due process and equal protection to the residents of all states. Yet its second section directs that states which deny the right to vote to any male citizens over the age of 21 will lose electors for president and vice president (in proportion that those denied the right bear to the whole number of such citizens)—except when such denial is "for participation in rebellion, or other crime."

The Supreme Court has held that this apparent recognition of the legitimacy of felon disenfranchisement in the 14th Amendment insulates the practice against constitutional attack. Even the 13th Amendment, which abolished slavery and

The Arguments Against Felon Voting Are Strong

Even if Congress had authority to pass the DRA [Democracy Restoration Act], it should not. There are compelling arguments in favor of disenfranchising felons—certainly strong enough to refute a claim that Congress must intervene to prevent some sort of irrational malfeasance in the states by dictating a one-size-fits-all national policy. Conversely, the policy arguments in favor of enfranchising felons are unpersuasive.

Those who are not willing to follow the law cannot claim a right to make the law for everyone else. And when you vote, you are indeed making the law—either directly, in a ballot initiative or referendum, or indirectly, by choosing lawmakers.

Not everyone in the United States may vote—not children, for example, or noncitizens, or the mentally incompetent, or criminals. We have certain minimum, objective standards of responsibility, trustworthiness, and commitment to our laws for those who would participate in the solemn enterprise of self-government. And it is not unreasonable to suppose that those who have committed serious crimes against their fellow citizens may be presumed—until they have shown otherwise—to lack this responsibility, trustworthiness, and commitment. Should children be voting? The mentally incompetent? People who are not citizens? People who refuse to follow the law and harm their fellow citizens? Of course not.

Roger Clegg, "Resolved, Congress Should Pass the Democracy Restoration Act Restoring the Right to Vote in Federal Elections to People with Criminal Records," Debating Reform: Conflicting Perspectives on How to Fix the American Political System. *Eds. Richard J. Ellis and Michael Nelson. Los Angeles, CA: Sage/CQ Press, 2014.*

involuntary servitude generally, carves out an exception "for crime whereof the party shall have been duly convicted."

That view, to be sure, has its critics, and their arguments are worth considering. For example, they argue that it is one thing to say that states cannot be denied electors for disenfranchising criminals, and quite another to say that the practice otherwise passes muster.

They note that the 14th Amendment's accommodation of gender-based voting distinction—using the population of 21-year-old male citizens as the measure—itself has been overtaken by history. Still, a fair reply would be that it took a constitutional amendment, the 19th, to do it.

The historical evidence suggests that even Reconstruction progressives saw the 14th Amendment's reference to gender as a political necessity and believed that the crime exception was principled. The concern that former slaves would be disenfranchised for trivial offenses was dealt with in the Military Reconstruction Act of 1867, which confined the sanction to felonies—serious crimes.

Rather than deal directly with the evidence, both statistical and historical, Mr. Holder put the issue squarely in terms of race: Because blacks stand convicted of crimes in greater numbers than their proportion of the population would dictate, the effect on them of felon disenfranchisement statutes is disproportionately high; that disproportion is unjust, and the laws should be repealed. The attorney general proposes substituting for current laws and practice what is essentially a transactional standard implicit in the phrase paying one's debt to society: Once the sentence has been served, the fine paid, it is time to make it—as a cleanup-company slogan says—like it never even happened.

Mr. Holder does not urge that we go as far as the states of Maine and Vermont, which bar disenfranchisement on any basis and thus permit convicts to vote from jail (assuming their residency requirements are otherwise in order). But neither does he display anything but contempt for the notion that there is a moral taint that attaches to a felony conviction—a taint that should require that one at least show some brief period of law-abiding existence before full readmission to the polity.

This failure actually hurts his case, because it invites cynicism about his motives. Thus a report in the *Washington Post* ended by citing an academic study showing that if disenfranchised felons had voted in the 2000 election, Al Gore would have been president. That may be true, but it probably doesn't help the attorney general's argument as much as sticking to the facts might have.

> "Once kids have reached the age where they begin to assume responsibility for themselves in other portions of life, they should be able to vote as well."

Birthright

Jonathan Bernstein

Jonathan Bernstein is a political scientist, a Bloomberg View columnist, and the coeditor of The Making of the Presidential Candidates 2012. *In the following viewpoint, he argues that children should have the right to vote from birth, with parents voting for them until they are in high school and then getting the ability to cast their own ballots. He points out that adults are not disenfranchised because of ignorance or lack of education; therefore, there is no reason to disenfranchise children for those reasons. In addition, he says that US democracy is based on interest politics, and children have interests just like everyone else. It is unlikely that having children vote would heavily affect elections, since they would not all vote for a single candidate. However, letting children vote would affirm the principles of American democracy and might encourage higher voting participation throughout life.*

As you read, consider the following questions:

1. According to Bernstein, why has the history of America not actually been one of a triumph of universal suffrage?

2. Why does Bernstein say that we have elections?

3. What would be the practical effects of children's voting, according to Bernstein?

In some interpretations of the history of the franchise in the United States, the story has been one of moving gradually, sometimes painfully so, away from limits on who could vote: Over time, property restrictions were dropped, then ethnicity (de jure), then gender, then ethnicity (de facto), with even the minimum age dropping to 18 after the passage and ratification of the 26th Amendment forty years ago this spring. While there have been some exceptions to this overall trend—for example, voting was made more difficult by voter registration laws during the Progressive Era and, more recently, the disenfranchisement of felons and even ex-felons—most Americans would agree that the basic story is one of the triumph of universal suffrage. But that's not actually the case. Millions of Americans are regularly disenfranchised because they have not reached the minimum required age.

While the question might sound preposterous at first, a fairly good case can be made for a system that I would term "vote-from-birth," in which age limits on voting would be eliminated entirely. Not only would older teens be allowed to vote independently, but parents would be responsible for casting votes on behalf of those too young to do so for themselves. Even if you don't ultimately buy into the idea, a thorough working through of the logic behind it proves helpful in parsing out some pretty basic questions about our belief in democracy.

Perhaps you're thinking at this point: Surely, teenagers are too ill-informed to cast votes. But we don't restrict the vote based on wisdom or on knowledge of the political system for current voters, including those who never finished high school or are otherwise unlikely to make wise choices. I think we're quite right not to do so, and to remember that ignorance as the stated grounds for restricting the ballot has been a common and unfortunate thread in American history. Indeed, once kids have reached the age where they begin to assume responsibility for themselves in other portions of life, they should be able to vote as well. For argument's sake, I'd set it at 15, the age they begin high school and a new level of independence, but I'd be open to arguments for a lower or slightly higher limit as well.

But what about even younger kids, for whom parents, under the vote-from-birth system, would cast votes by proxy? To make the case for this, it's necessary to begin with a more basic question: Why do we have elections to begin with? What, in other words, is the advantage of democracy? One of the strongest justifications for democracy is to aggregate interests. And, if democracy is at least partly about aggregating interests, the case for voting from birth is surprisingly strong.

Under this rationale for democracy, the reason for elections has to do with a self-interest, then policy decisions will eventually reflect their accumulated will, at least to some extent, or much better at least than if some autocratic or technocratic government made the decisions. We alone know, and judge, our own interests.

But children, even infants, have interests that are as legitimate as those of anyone else. Indeed, when we take the census and calculate congressional district apportionment and other formulas, children count just as much as adults. It's true, of course, that for young children, parents would have to exercise that vote on their behalf, but that's hardly a big deal; we expect parents to do all sorts of things on behalf of the interests

Do Parents Vote for Children?

Children are counted in apportionment. Should they be? Who represents children? Who votes for children? Do all parents vote for policies that benefit all children? Do all parents vote? Professor Elizabeth Cohen suggests parents do not necessarily vote in the best interest of their children: "Parents are expected to represent children at the ballot box when, in fact, it is likely that the interests of those children may run contrary to the interests of their parents. School improvements mean higher taxes for parents, not all of whom are willing to sacrifice for their children. Or parents may not vote at all (many don't)."

Do parents use their added voting power to increase public spending on education while cutting spending on health care for the elderly? Will parents sacrifice the needs of grandparents? Parents can deceive themselves into thinking that what is in their own best interest is also in their child's best interest: "While raising children may involve a degree of selflessness unimaginable to the childless, it is also true that few parents can see the degree to which they impose conceptions of 'best interests' on their children because those conceptions suit their own (adult) interests." Do parents in wealthy communities vote to fund health care and day care programs for children in low-income communities? Will fixed-income retirees vote to fund schools adequately?

Orlando J. Rodriguez,
Vote Thieves: Illegal Immigration Redistricting, and
Presidential Elections. *Washington, DC: Potomac Books, 2011.*

of their children. As for the objection that this would unfairly give parents "extra" votes, that's only the case if one thinks of children as non-people. Otherwise, parents are only getting their own votes, plus children are getting theirs, and that's only natural.

Setting theory aside for a minute, what would be the practical effects on the political landscape of vote-from-birth? Probably nothing too revolutionary. Parents with young children would, of course, have a bit more weight in the political system; those who argue that older people (who have relatively high participation rates) are overrepresented might like that. Older children and teenagers might continue to simply vote alongside their parents—or, perhaps, if they had to show up at the polls themselves, they might have even lower turn-out rates than their 18- to 25-year-old brothers and sisters, who have the lowest rates of any current group. As far as partisan balance, if the National Scholastic quadrennial vote-in-school program is any indication, kids pretty much echo whatever the broader electorate does. On the good side, it is perhaps plausible that making voting more of a family activity could encourage and even enrich participation, as parents might benefit from explaining their choices to their children, and children could get hands-on experience with the basics of democracy while they are still living at home, in intermediate range (say, ages 8 through 14) in which children were required to be at the polls when parents cast votes on their behalf.

In the end, if American democracy is understood at least partly as a matter of interest aggregation, then the case for everyone voting makes a lot of sense. In fact, there's little doubt in my mind that if things had evolved a bit differently and we currently had vote-from-birth, no one would even dream of stripping away this right. Although Republicans might, I suppose, want to require long-form birth certificates at the polling place.

> *"For disability advocates, measures that make political participation harder for people with disabilities are particularly troubling with the future of Medicaid at stake."*

People with Mental Disabilities Should Have the Right to Vote

Deanna Pan

Deanna Pan is a former senior editorial fellow at Mother Jones. *In the following viewpoint, she reports that mentally disabled people in Arizona who live under a guardian's care can gain the right to vote if they petition the court and a judge determines that they have a "sufficient understanding to exercise the right to vote." Pan says that this is a step forward, but she argues that it will still disenfranchise many of the mentally disabled, preventing them from voting on issues such as Medicaid and federal funding that directly affect them. She adds that there is no evidence that allowing the mentally disabled to vote increases voter fraud. She concludes that barriers to voting for the mentally disabled should be rolled back.*

As you read, consider the following questions:

1. Who is Clinton Gode, and why was his right to vote restricted, according to Pan?

2. In 2008, what percentage of people with disabilities voted, and how does this compare to nondisabled voters, according to the viewpoint?

3. What personal experience does Gode cite as a reason for wanting to vote, according to Pan?

Three months ago, Clinton Gode testified before an Arizona probate judge, explaining how he got his news, why he wants to vote in tomorrow's election, and which presidential candidate he prefers.

Targeting the Disabled

The judge asked if people ever try to tell him how to vote. "Yeah," Gode replied, "but I don't listen to them."

That was a fine answer. After a half an hour of this line of questioning, Judge Lee Jantzen of the Mohave County Superior Court banged his gavel and granted Gode the right to vote.

Gode, who is 25, has Down syndrome. When he was 18, his parents became his legal guardians so they could manage his medical and financial affairs, which disqualified him from voting in Arizona. Now, Gode will cast a ballot on Tuesday [November 2012] thanks to a new state law that allows people with court-appointed guardians to petition for and restore their suffrage if a judge determines "by clear and convincing evidence" that they have "sufficient understanding to exercise the right to vote."

House Bill 2377 passed overwhelmingly in the Arizona legislature last April, with Gode as its official spokesperson. It was lauded as a compromise between Republican lawmakers and disability advocates, who had been fighting for more than a decade to enfranchise Arizonans under guardianship.

Arizona is one of 14 states that categorically bar people who are under guardianship or are judged to be mentally "incompetent" or "incapacitated" from voting, according to the Bazelon Center for Mental Health Law. Although all but 11 states have disability-related voting restrictions, laws that impose uniform bans on people who are under guardianship or judged to be incompetent disproportionately target adults with disabilities or mental illness, including veterans with traumatic brain injury, seniors with dementia, and people with autism.

These laws are "inherently biased" and violate constitutional guarantees of equal protection and due process, says Lewis Bossing, a senior staff attorney at the Bazelon Center. They're "based on a faulty stereotype" that "people with mental disabilities can't make decisions, don't have a preference in a political issue or among political candidates, or can't express that preference in a way that is reliable."

Vote Fraud Worries Overblown

Supporters of voter competence requirements say these measures are necessary to prevent voter fraud. They worry that caregivers or poll workers could improperly coerce vulnerable adults to vote a certain way. Minnesota state representative Mary Kiffmeyer made a similar argument earlier this year. The Republican lawmaker, who is also spearheading her state's voter ID amendment, sponsored a bill in February to limit the voting rights of Minnesotans under guardianship. Kiffmeyer, who is the legal guardian of her disabled sister, cited a 2010 incident in which a group of adults with mental disabilities allegedly cast ballots with improper assistance from their caregivers. An investigation into the allegations turned up no evidence of illegal voter manipulation.

After Kiffmeyer's bill stalled, a group of conservative activists took up her cause as part of a wide-ranging federal lawsuit to ensure that ballots cast by ineligible voters, such as felons and wards of the state, aren't counted. The case was dismissed in August; the plaintiffs have filed an appeal.

The new Arizona law isn't a perfect solution for people like Gode. Studies show that people with disabilities are often sidelined from the political process. In 2008, 46.1 percent of people with disabilities voted, compared with 64.5 percent of their fellow nondisabled citizens. Voter ID restrictions also pose an undue burden on them because securing proper documentation can be expensive and impractical. Inaccessible polling places also keep disabled voters from casting their ballots. And even when people with disabilities do get their voting rights restored, they must jump through legal hoops like those Gode did. "This is a barrier to voting most people don't face," says Bossing.

Medicaid

For disability advocates, measures that make political participation harder for people with disabilities are particularly troubling with the future of Medicaid at stake. More than 44 percent of people with disabilities depend on Medicaid. [Republican presidential candidate] Mitt Romney has promised to repeal the Affordable Care Act [officially known as the Patient Protection and Affordable Care Act, or Obamacare] and turn Medicaid into a block grant program run by the states. "Block grants would end up pitting children who need health care against older individuals who want to stay in their homes against people with disabilities who want to live in communities," says Bruce Darling, president of the Center for Disability Rights. "It's going to be a terrible game of who's going to be able to make their case and who has the most political power."

Clinton Gode has seen what happens when publicly funded programs are squeezed dry. A year and a half ago, state budget cuts forced him to move out of his group home in Kingman, Arizona. "I was in a group home and my house [was] not doing so good for money-wise," Gode recalls. "And then somebody came in and . . . said to me, 'You need to move out because budget cuts.'"

That's why Gode is voting on Tuesday. "Budget cuts affect everybody," he says. With the help of his parents, Gode found a studio apartment run by a local nonprofit in Lake Havasu City.

On Tuesday, his parents will drive him to his polling place, where he'll cast his vote for the presidential candidate he hopes will help him and his friends continue to live as independently as possible. "I have been reading about Barack Obama," he says. "I want to vote. I'm really, really happy I vote right now, and I'm so excited."

> *"Even if we used to exclude many citizens for bad reasons, there might be good reasons to exclude many citizens from holding power."*

Incompetent Voters Should Not Be Allowed to Vote

Jason Brennan

Jason Brennan is an assistant professor at Georgetown University. In the following viewpoint, he argues that it is unjust for a citizen to be subjected to the decisions of people who are incompetent, unjust, or immoral. Many people who vote, he says, are incompetent, unjust, or immoral and thus exercise unjust power over others. He says that to diminish this injustice, the vote should be restricted to people who are competent and intelligent. Elite voting may not be perfect, he says, but it would be more just than the system currently used in the United States.

As you read, consider the following questions:

1. What is an epistocracy, according to Brennan?

2. How does Brennan describe an ignorant jury?

Jason Brennan, "The Right to a Competent Electorate," *Philosophical Quarterly*, October 2011, pp. 700–724. Copyright © 2011 by Oxford University Press Journals. All rights reserved. Reproduced by permission.

3. What example does Brennan provide of an instance in which bad voting was disastrous?

In this [viewpoint], I argue that the practice of unrestricted, universal suffrage is unjust. Citizens have a right that any political power held over them should be exercised by competent people in a competent way. In realistic circumstances, universal suffrage violates this right. Since nearly all current democracies have universal suffrage, all current democracies are to that extent unjust.

The Unjust Mob

Many of my fellow citizens are incompetent, ignorant, irrational, and morally unreasonable about politics. Despite that, they hold political power over me. These can staff offices of great power and wield the coercive authority of the state against me. They can force me to do things I do not wish to do, or have no good reason to do.

As an innocent person, I should not have to tolerate that. Just as it would be wrong to force me to go under the knife of an incompetent surgeon, or to sail with an incompetent ship captain, it is wrong to force me to submit to the decisions of incompetent voters. People who exercise power over me—including other voters—should have to do so in a competent and morally reasonable way. Otherwise, as a matter of justice, they ought to be excluded from holding political power, including the power to vote. Or so I will argue.

In modern democracies, we grant every adult citizen a legal right to vote. (Some democracies exclude some citizens, such as felons or the insane.) We used to restrict people from voting for morally arbitrary reasons, such as skin color or sex. This practice was unjust. Still, even if we used to exclude many citizens for bad reasons, there might be good reasons to exclude many citizens from holding power. In parallel, consider that it would be unjust to exclude citizens from driving because they are atheists. However, even if that law would be unjust, it would not follow that all restrictions on the legal right to drive would be unjust. So it might be with political rights as well. Democracies used to exclude citizens from holding power for bad reasons, but perhaps they should begin excluding citizens for good reasons.

Elite Democracy

In this [viewpoint], I argue on behalf of restricted suffrage. I argue that it is unjust to grant certain citizens the legal right to exercise political power over others. I argue that a form of epistocracy with restricted suffrage is morally superior to democracy with unconditional universal suffrage. Broadly speaking, a polity is epistocratic to the extent that knowledge and competence are legal requirements for holding political power. Plato advocated rule by philosopher kings, an extreme form of epistocracy. All modern democracies exclude children from voting and holding office on grounds that the children are incompetent. In that sense, all democracies are weakly epistocratic. In this [viewpoint], I argue for a moderate epistocratic position. I argue that in contemporary democracies, citizens should have to possess sufficient moral and epistemic competence in order to have the right to vote.

I am thus arguing for what we might call an *elite electoral system*. Elite electoral systems have political mechanisms similar to those found in contemporary democracies, but restrict electoral power to citizens who can demonstrate competence. Elite electoral systems are moderately epistocratic. Note, however, that I will not argue that a moderate epistocracy—or any kind of epistocracy—is the *most* or *ideally* just form of government. My goal is limited: I want to argue that, all things remaining equal, in contemporary democracies, restricted suffrage would be a *moral improvement* over unconditional universal suffrage. That said, restricted suffrage might still itself be unjust—better than universal suffrage, but not good enough to qualify as just. Restricted suffrage might be unjust, but *less unjust* than unconditional universal suffrage. . . .

The Basic Argument for Restricted Suffrage

I argue that universal suffrage is unjust, because it violates a citizen's right not to be subject to high-stakes decisions made by incompetent and morally unreasonable people. In later sections, I argue that restricted suffrage is morally superior to universal suffrage.

Philosophers and laypeople sometimes assert that anyone subject to political power ought to have a say in how that power is wielded. Granting a citizen political power might to some degree reconcile her to her own government, as it reduces the degree to which government is an imposition upon her. However, the right to vote not only gives a citizen a say over herself, but also a say over other people. We have basic rights to govern and decide for ourselves, but no basic rights to govern or decide for others. We do not have any basic right to run other people's lives or to impose rules upon them.

Democracy is, among other things, a particular kind of decision-making method. *Political* democracy is, among other things, a method for deciding when, how, and in what ways a government will threaten people with violence in order to induce compliance with rules. To possess the right to vote is to possess some degree of political power, however small. This power is held over *others*, not just over oneself.

Democracy with unconditional universal suffrage grants political power in a promiscuous way. When an ignorant, misinformed, morally unreasonable, or irrational citizen votes, he exercises political power over others, and this cries out for justification. In particular, it needs to be justified against an otherwise identical system in which politically incompetent and unreasonable citizens are excluded from voting.

The Competence Principle
and Jury Analogy

The basic rationale for restricted suffrage can be illustrated by analogy to a jury trial. In criminal cases, juries hold serious power over defendants. The jury's decision can significantly alter the defendant's life prospects, and deprive him of property, liberty, and life.

Consider these three hypothetical juries.

1. *The Ignorant Jury*: The jurists pay no attention during the trial. When asked to deliberate, they are ignorant of the details of the case, but find the defendant guilty anyway. After the trial, they admit they decided the case this way (or we have some other strong source of evidence that this is how they made their decision).

2. *The Irrational Jury*: The jurists pay some attention to the details of the case. However, they find the defendant guilty not on the basis of the evidence, but on the basis of wishful thinking and various bizarre conspiracy theories they happen to believe. After the trial, they admit they decided the case this way (or we have some other strong source of evidence that this is how they made their decision).

3. *The Morally Unreasonable Jury*: The jurists find the defendant guilty because he is Muslim, and they are Christians who think Muslims pervert the Word of God. After the trial, they admit they decided the case this way (or we have some other strong source of evidence that this is how they made their decision).

These juries lack authority and legitimacy. (A jury has authority over a defendant when the defendant has a moral obligation to abide by the jury's decision, *because* it is the jury's decision. A jury has legitimacy over a defendant when it is morally permissible for the government to enforce the jury's decision against the defendant.) If a defendant knew he had been subject to one of these juries, he would have no moral obligation to regard decisions as authoritative. It would be unjust for a government to knowingly enforce these decisions—enforcement would deprive a citizen of property, liberty, and/or life for unacceptable reasons, on the basis of an improperly made decision.

The Competence Principle:

It is unjust to deprive a citizen of life, liberty, or property, or to significantly alter her life prospects by force and threats of force, as a result of decisions made by an incompetent or morally unreasonable deliberative body, or as a result of decisions made in an incompetent and morally unreasonable way.

In the case of jury trials, it is plausible that defendants have a right to a competent jury, expressed as follows.

The Competence Principle disqualifies jurists who have sufficiently bad epistemic and moral character (even though people of overall bad character might act competently in particular cases). It also disqualifies individual jury decisions (even if the jury overall has good epistemic and moral character) when these decisions are made badly. The Competence Principle implies

1. that people of bad epistemic and moral character should not be jurists at all, and,

2. when it is known that particular decisions were made incompetently (even if the decisions were made by people who are generally competent and reasonable), these decisions should not be enforced, and defendants have no duty to submit to them.

In short, the Competence Principle requires each decision of a certain sort to be made competently by competent people.

We could not justify enforcing an incompetent jury decision by showing that most juries are competent. The defendant can object that in his case, the jury was not. We cannot deprive him of liberty, property, or life on the basis of an incompetent decision just because *other* juries are competent. . . .

To some degree, the United States attempts to abide by the Competence Principle with regard to jury decisions. Potential jurors are selected at random from all adult citizens within a geographic area. However, individual jurors are sometimes disqualified because they exhibit bias or certain kinds of incompetence. In law, because criminal convictions can deprive defendants of property, liberty, and (sometimes) life, defendants are entitled to a fair trial by an impartial jury. After a trial, if it becomes known that the jury made its decision in a corrupt or incompetent way, as in the three cases above, this can be legal grounds for overturning the jury's decision.

Applying the Competence Principle to Government

The Competence Principle has a broad scope of application. It does not merely apply to jury decisions.

Democratic governments, like juries, also can deprive citizens (and others) of property, liberty, and life. Indeed, they often do. Democratic governments can impose policies that significantly alter citizens' life prospects for the worse. If defendants are entitled to competent juries, there might be similar reasons to hold that citizens are entitled to competent governments.

If a police officer, judge, or politician makes a capricious, irrational, or malicious decision, a citizen cannot walk away. In general, the citizen may choose either to submit to the decision, or be penalized (through coercion) for noncompliance. (Sometimes, if she is lucky, she can obtain a remedy after the fact.)

Governments do more than choose flag colors and melodies for national anthems. They make policies and choose courses of action that can have momentous and even disastrous consequences for citizens. For example, if a central bank or treasury pursues bad monetary policies, and if the government imposes high trade barriers, this can push a recession into a deep depression. If military leaders inflate or misrepresent the evidence given to them by intelligence agencies, this can induce a costly, destructive, and inhumane war.

Governmental decisions tend to have two crucial features:

1. The outcomes of decisions are imposed involuntarily through violence and threats of violence. Citizens and others within the government's domain are forced to comply, even if they have excellent grounds for noncompliance, and even if they know that the decisions were made incompetently.

2. Governmental decisions tend to be of major significance. They can significantly alter the life prospects of citizens, and deprive them of life, liberty, and property.

In light of 1 and 2, citizens may demand competence from government officials and decision makers as a matter of right. Unfortunately, this right is often and perhaps almost always unenforceable, but to possess a right does not require that it be enforceable. After all, when [Adolf] Hitler and [Joseph] Stalin murdered millions of people, we would say that Hitler and Stalin thus violated their rights to life, even though these people lacked effective enforcement of these rights. To say that citizens may demand competence from government officials and decision makers as a matter of right is to say that, prima facie, incompetent decision making or having decisions made by incompetent people is unjust.

The Competence Principle applies not merely to juries, but to others who hold political power, such as the police, bureaucrats and ministers, judges, and politicians holding public office. To some degree, in practice, governments attempt to abide by the Competence Principle. Many positions of power require certain qualifications from applicants in order to obtain that power. We do not make just anyone a police officer, nor can just anyone run the Fed [referring to the Federal Reserve System]. Judges must have law degrees, and even politicians are often subject to requirements. These requirements are imposed to eliminate gross incompetence.

Applying the Competence Principle to the Electorate

In democracies, the ultimate holders of power are voters. Generally, voters determine how political offices will be staffed. Voters choose rulers, who then wield the coercive power of the state against innocent citizens, including citizens who justifiably oppose the state's actions. If voters choose badly, the consequences can be dire.

We should not understate the damage bad voting can do. Bad voting can be and has been disastrous. Even if in the U.S. or the U.K. disastrous candidates rarely have a chance of winning, we should not forget that many disastrous candidates have been elected to power in other parts of the world. The voters who put the National Socialists [Nazis] in power in Germany in 1933 cannot be held responsible for everything their government did. But much of what their government did was foreseeable by any reasonably well-informed person, and so their supporters were blameworthy.

Despite bad voting, we might still get good policies, and we might get bad policies despite good voting. Still, voting does make a difference. In general, the lower the epistemic and moral quality of the electorate, the worse governmental policies will tend to be. Low-quality electorates will tend to make worse choices at the polls—they will be worse at selecting good leaders, and will tend to choose worse policies during referenda. Having a low-quality electorate also tends to reduce the quality of the candidates who appear on the ballot. A low-quality electorate rigs the quality of an election's results downward even before the election takes place.

The Competence Principle applies equally well to the electorate as to juries. Consider these three hypothetical electorates:

1. *The Ignorant Electorate*: The majority of voters pay no attention to the details of the election, or the issues at stake. During the election, they choose a particular candidate at random. They admit they decided the election this way (or we have some other strong source of evidence that this is how they made their decision).

2. *The Irrational Electorate*: The majority pay some attention to the details of the election and the issues at stake. However, they vote not on the basis of evidence, but on the basis of wishful thinking and various disreputable social scientific theories they happen to believe. They admit they decided the election this way (or we have some other strong source of evidence that this is how they made their decision).

3. *The Morally Unreasonable Electorate*: Simply out of racism, the majority choose a white candidate over a black candidate. They admit they decided the election this way (or we have some other strong source of evidence that this is how they made their decision).

Suppose, in each of these cases, the majority do not represent everyone in society. For instance, there might be some well-informed, rational, and morally reasonable minority voters, or there may be innocent nonvoters, such as children or resident aliens. If so, then majority voters have done something deeply unjust—they have imposed a ruler on innocent people without having adequate grounds for its decision. (Note also that if voters tend to be ignorant, irrational, or morally unreasonable, this will not only tend to result in bad choices at the polls, but also tend to make it so that the candidates printed on the ballot are of lower quality in the first place.)

The governed have a right not to be exposed to undue risk in the selection of policy or of rulers who will make policy. When elections are decided on the basis of unreliable epistemic procedures or on the basis of unreasonable moral attitudes, this exposes the governed to undue risk of serious harm. Since the governed are *forced* to comply with the decisions of the electorate, negligent decision making is intolerable. The electorate has an obligation to the governed not to expose them to undue risk.

This concludes the basic argument for restricted suffrage. When high-stakes decisions are imposed upon innocent people, the Competence Principle requires every individual decision to be made competently and reasonably by competent and reasonable people. It applies not merely to jury decisions, but to any significant decision made by those holding political power.

Periodical and Internet Sources Bibliography

The following articles have been selected to supplement the diverse views presented in this chapter.

Associated Press	"Holder Urges Restoring Voting Rights to Ex-Inmates," *CBS News*, February 11, 2014.
Guy Benson	"Fraud: Local NBC Investigation Discovers Dozens of Illegal Voters in Florida," Townhall.com, March 19, 2014.
Harry J. Enten	"Why Is No One Fighting for the Voting Rights of Prisoners and Ex-Prisoners?," AlterNet, July 31, 2013.
David Horowitz	"Democrats Groom the Mentally Disabled to Vote," Newsmax, November 23, 2012.
Huffington Post	"Here's How Often Undocumented Immigrants Commit Voter Fraud in Arizona," November 18, 2013.
Michael Laris	"Voting-Rights Quest in Va. Will Become Easier for Ex-Prisoners Held on Serious Drug Charges," *Washington Post*, April 18, 2014.
Michael McLaughlin	"Felon Voting Laws Disenfranchise 5.85 Million Americans with Criminal Records: The Sentencing Project," *Huffington Post*, July 12, 2012.
Jim Ragsdale	"Hot Dish Politics: Felons' Rights All Over the Map," *Star Tribune* (Minneapolis, MN), April 12, 2014.
Maya Rhodan	"Obama Administration Seeks Voting Rights for Former Inmates," *Time*, February 11, 2014.
Francis Wilkinson	"When Immigrant Voter Fraud Was Real," *Bloomberg View*, May 1, 2014.

Can Changing Voting Procedures Promote Fairness and Equality?

Chapter Preface

One way in which some states have tried to promote voter registration and increase equal access to the polls is through registering an individual to vote when he or she applies for a driver's license.

The National Voter Registration Act of 1993, or the Motor Voter Act, requires employees at state motor vehicle departments to ask all those who apply for a driver's license if they would like to register to vote or to update their voter information. However, states have in some cases taken additional steps to register voters at driver's license facilities. For instance, in 2010 Texas automated the link between motor vehicle offices and the secretary of state, so that voter registration information could be sent electronically, according to Steven Rosenfeld in a May 24, 2010, article at the Project Vote website.

Other states have been even more ambitious. Montgomery County in Maryland, for instance, is considering a measure to automatically register all drivers to vote. "If passed, Maryland's voter registration policy would change from an 'opt-in' system—where people are asked if they would like to register—to an 'opt-out' system, where they would be registered to vote unless they asked not to be," explained Glynis Kazanjian in a November 25, 2013, post at MarylandReporter.com.

Oregon also has contemplated moving to automatic registration. Oregon secretary of state Kate Brown has advocated for the change, arguing that it will register some six hundred thousand new voters, according to Nigel Jaquiss in a June 12, 2013, article in the *Willamette Week*. However, the bill has been stalled because of partisan resistance. Republicans worry that a majority of new voters would be Democratic, since Democrats do disproportionately well among poor and minority voters who may find it difficult to register. Oregon Republican Party spokesman Greg Leo was quoted by Jaquiss as saying, "what this bill would do is allow Democrats to rebuild the kind of registration advantage they had before the 2008 election." In reply, Paul Gronke, chairman of the Political Science Department at Reed College, said, "Republicans should try to appeal to Hispanics rather than try to keep them off the rolls."

The authors of the viewpoints in the following chapter debate other technical changes to voting, including bilingual ballots, early voting, and ranked-choice voting.

> *"Modernizing registration alone will not eliminate long voting lines. But combined with the voting commission's ideas, we can fix the problems that led to them in the first place."*

A Bipartisan Path to Fixing America's Broken Elections

Michael Waldman

Michael Waldman is president of the Brennan Center for Justice at New York University School of Law, a nonpartisan law and policy institute that focuses on improving the systems of democracy and justice. In the following viewpoint, he congratulates a bipartisan commission that suggested voting reforms. These reforms include modernizing election systems and moving voter registration to computer rather than using the error-prone method of pen and paper. The commission also said that early voting should be available for all citizens. Waldman says that these are valuable recommendations and encourages states and Congress to enact them into law.

As you read, consider the following questions:

1. Who does Waldman say blocked the worst state voting restrictions?

2. What does Waldman say is the underlying cause of Election Day chaos in the United States?

3. What congressional bill already exists to modernize elections, and who are its sponsors, according to the viewpoint?

One year ago, in his State of the Union address, President [Barack] Obama decried the long lines that marred the 2012 election. Winding up for a major proposal, he announced the creation of ... a commission. Sigh. Everyone knows that in Washington, when you want an issue to go away, convene a panel. That's where ideas go to die.

Worthy Recommendations

This week [in January 2014] we got a surprise: This commission may well have been worth the effort. Comprised of hard-charging partisan election lawyers from both major parties, and corporate experts on efficiency and consumer satisfaction, the panel released its recommendations Wednesday. They set out a strong set of "best practices" to modernize and improve the ramshackle way our democracy runs elections. The panel's work offers the best chance in ages to burst past the partisan stalemate on voting issues.

Few topics have been as enmeshed in hyper-partisanship. Over the past four years, Republicans in state capitols have pressed to enact two dozen laws that cumulatively would have made it harder for millions to vote. The worst were blocked by courts—federal, state, GOP-appointed, Democrat-appointed. In June of last year [2013], the most partisan court in the country, the Supreme Court, weighed in, gutting the Voting Rights Act. Democrats shouted "voter suppression;" Republicans warned of "fraud."

Meanwhile, as we saw in 2012, even when the worst voting laws were frozen by courts, far too many citizens found themselves up against the creaky electoral machinery. In Florida and other states, voters had to wait in line for hours to cast a ballot. Changes in early voting rules made it worse. At last year's address to Congress, President Obama highlighted the story of a 102-year-old woman who waited three hours to cast her ballot.

The panel's recommendations are a significant first step to solve the problem, and one reason the commission's words will carry weight is the pedigree of its chairmen. Bob Bauer, a former White House counsel, was the Obama campaign's lawyer in both election cycles. Ben Ginsberg is the top Republican election lawyer, well known for his role in the 2000 Florida recount. (Bob Balaban played him in the HBO movie.) He was [Republican presidential candidate] Mitt Romney's top lawyer. No RINOs or DINOs [Republicans in Name Only and Democrats in Name Only] here.

Modernization Needed

The commissioners looked at the electoral mess, and concluded that strong steps should be taken to avoid further fiascos. They start by recognizing that the underlying cause of Election Day chaos is our antiquated, paper-based voter registration system. In the age of smartphones and tablets, most Americans still register to vote using ink-and-paper form. Illegible handwriting and typos lead to errors and duplicate entries. These voter roll problems create havoc on Election Day. The panel embraced some of the innovations now flowering in states, including online registration and electronically transferring data from the Department of Motor Vehicles to statewide voter lists. These are among the steps needed to truly modernize the system.

The panel also addressed some more divisive topics. Take early voting, which is wildly popular and which eases long lines on Election Day itself. In 2012, some states, including Florida, cut back on early voting, with predictably unsettling results. The panel declared that early voting should be available to all citizens. This implicitly rebukes North Carolina as it moves to cut back on early balloting as part of its wildly controversial plan. (Not to mention illegal, and unconstitutional, in my view.) The commissioners also declared that no voter should have to wait more than a half hour. That will now be a powerful national benchmark.

The panel left some things out. It did not embrace all the most effective reforms to modernize voter registration, a step that would protect against fraud while registering millions. And the commissioners wisely left untouched the most contentious issues, such as voter identification laws. Still, in all, it could be a breakthrough package.

Such reforms could easily gather dust, lodged on the shelf in between the last "how to reform entitlements" and "the need for infrastructure spending" commissions. So it's up to state governments, especially, to take the cue and implement reforms.

Up to the States

In fact, despite the harsh fights over voting laws, many states have quietly moved to expand voter registration and modernize electoral systems. In 2013, more states passed laws to improve voting than to restrict it. Now governors and legislators should embrace the Bauer-Ginsberg package of changes. Already, a mobilized citizen movement to advance voting reform is ready to push. States with the best chance for action include Massachusetts and Connecticut.

And the report makes clear by implication that voting is a national concern. Minimum national standards are essential. And that means, in the end, national legislation to ensure that states take responsibility to expand voting access and modern-

Long Lines and Discrimination

While Americans were proud of the historic turnout in some places and among certain groups on Election Day, the amount of time some citizens had to wait in order to vote was not just an unfortunate consequence of increased voter participation. The delay at many polling places could have denied many voters their right to cast a ballot. While in many precincts voting took only a matter of minutes, in Detroit and St. Louis some voters had to wait in line for five hours. In the St. Louis area the longest wait was six hours. While the commitment of so many to wait no matter how long it took was inspiring, some voters inevitably could not wait that long. . . . And once again the distribution of resources, in terms of staffing and voting machines, was random at best and possibly discriminatory at worst. This problem was widely predicted by voting rights advocates, who warned that states did not have enough voting machines for the expected turnout and had no plans in place for ensuring that the machines available were allocated strategically and fairly. . . .

After the election, a team of researchers published a report on the performance of the election. They found that African American respondents to their survey reported waiting on long lines far more often than whites or Hispanics. Some 27 percent of African Americans reported long waits, compared with 11 percent of whites and 13 percent of Hispanics. The report found that 20 percent of African Americans waited more than half an hour to vote, compared with 14 percent of whites and 15 percent of Hispanics. This disparity in the efficiency of polling stations in predominantly black and white neighborhoods had been found in 2004 as well.

Tova Andrea Wang, The Politics of Voter Suppression:
Defending and Expanding Americans' Right to Vote.
Ithaca, NY: Cornell University Press, 2012.

ize elections. Congress—yes, that dysfunctional branch of government—can make it happen. None other than Justice Antonin Scalia says it's true.

In June, the Supreme Court made clear that Congress has a strong role to play in regulating federal elections. The opinion, written by Justice Scalia, invalidated an Arizona law making it harder to register.

A bill already exists to modernize elections on a national scale. Civil rights hero John Lewis (D-Ga.) and Sen. Kirsten Gillibrand (D-N.Y.) introduced the Voter Empowerment Act last year. It's full of ideas both Republicans and Democrats can get behind. Many of the commission's recommendations, in fact, mirror the legislative proposal.

That's something both parties can agree on—and they have. With little fanfare and partisan wrangling, 43 states have already adopted key elements of voter registration modernization. A national standard would energize reform across the country.

To be sure, modernizing registration alone will not eliminate long voting lines. But combined with the voting commission's ideas, we can fix the problems that led to them in the first place.

So let's give two and a half cheers for the commission's proposals. When Republicans and Democrats agree on key voting reforms, in an election year, that's a rare sign of hope.

| "*More voters coming to the polls usually means more Democratic voters.*"

Partisanship Will Prevent Equitable Voting Reform

Philip Bump

Philip Bump is a writer at the Wire, a news and opinion website. In the following viewpoint, he reports on bipartisan election recommendations from a presidential commission. He says that some of the commission's recommendations, such as expanded early voting, are useful. However, he says that everything involving voting is highly partisan, since Democrats tend to do better when voter turnout is high and Republicans therefore have an interest in reducing voter turnout and making voting more difficult. He concludes that, given the partisan interests of Republicans, there is unlikely to be any real movement forward on bipartisan voting reform.

As you read, consider the following questions:

1. Who is Desiline Victor, according to Bump?

2. What does Bump believe is a telling moment in the documentary *Mitt*?

3. What does Rick Hasen call a "time bomb," according to Bump?

Fixing the country's uneven and archaic voting system isn't complex: Expand voting times, use better data systems, share resources. But even a comprehensive and unbiased report from a presidential panel isn't likely to quickly sweep problems aside. Elections, after all, are all about politics.

Partisanship and Voting

During his 2013 State of the Union Address, President [Barack] Obama announced that he was forming a panel of experts, led by attorneys from each party, to develop recommendations that he hoped would ensure that voting problems that emerged during the 2012 election wouldn't be repeated. He invited 102-year-old Desiline Victor to be his guest, telling the audience that she had to wait three hours to vote in North Miami.

As data compiled by the *New York Times* last year showed, Florida was by far the most difficult state in which to vote in 2012, with an average wait time of 45 minutes. It was this sort of confusion and frustration that Obama hoped to curtail by forming the Presidential Commission on Election Administration, which revealed its findings on Wednesday [in January 2014].

The *Huffington Post*'s Ryan Reilly outlines the main recommendations of the group. "States should implement online voter registration and expand early voting in order to reduce long lines at the voting booth," the group found, given that "long lines were a bigger problem in larger jurisdictions and that nearly half of Americans lived in places where elections officials admitted long lines were an issue." The report includes a set of interesting tools like this wait-time simulator for polling places.

At the *Election Law Blog*, Rick Hasen says that the panel "accomplish[ed] much more than I thought could be accom-

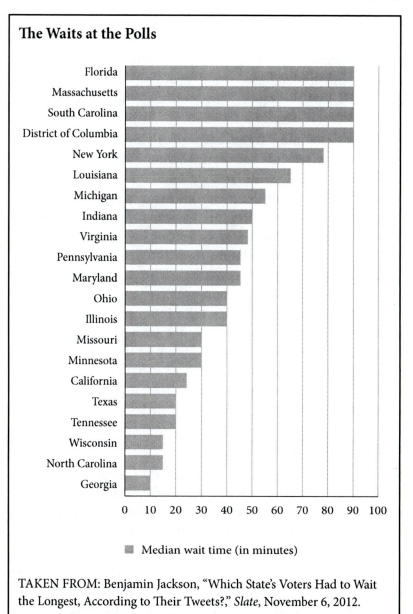

The Waits at the Polls

Florida
Massachusetts
South Carolina
District of Columbia
New York
Louisiana
Michigan
Indiana
Virginia
Pennsylvania
Maryland
Ohio
Illinois
Missouri
Minnesota
California
Texas
Tennessee
Wisconsin
North Carolina
Georgia

0   10   20   30   40   50   60   70   80   90   100

Median wait time (in minutes)

TAKEN FROM: Benjamin Jackson, "Which State's Voters Had to Wait the Longest, According to Their Tweets?," *Slate*, November 6, 2012.

plished given the limited charge." He points to six of the most important things that emerged from the group (whose full report can be seen here). First, that voter fraud is a negligible issue. "[T]here's not much in the report which is overly controversial," Hasen writes, which is in part because the focus on fraud as a threat to the sanctity of elections is highly partisan. Hasen's admiration of the group's ability to get something done is, he thinks, based on it avoiding such controversial topics. All that the report says, really, is that fraud, when it rarely occurs, is usually a function of absentee ballots.

But sidestepping fraud because it's political emphasizes why even the sensible recommendations of the group aren't likely to be seized upon by state legislatures. Early voting— which can, for example, mean allowing people to come to centralized polling places on weekends prior to Election Day—is a demonstrated way of getting more people to vote, and is a core recommendation from the panel. But in 2012 in Ohio it became a deeply contested issue. A few weeks before Election Day, early voting hours were curtailed in Democratic areas by the state's Republican legislature, prompting a raft of lawsuits. Ohio's secretary of state, who implemented the changes, eventually completed a survey of the 2012 election in the state, finding that fraud "is not an epidemic." Fraud, of course, was why the legislature insisted early voting restrictions were necessary.

Out of Date Technology

More voters coming to the polls usually means more Democratic voters. It's why Republicans usually fare better in non-presidential elections: Fewer people coming to the polls tends to mean that a higher percentage of them are Republicans. One of the most telling scenes in the upcoming Netflix documentary *Mitt* is when [Republican presidential candidate] Mitt Romney emerges from voting in Massachusetts that November to discuss with his wife how strong turnout appeared to be. He doesn't sound happy about it.

Which is why Republican legislatures, the primary drivers of new voting restrictions in 14 states since 2011, likely won't feel compelled by the commission's findings to leap into action to make it easier to vote.

As Hasen notes, there's another contentious issue in the report's recommendations, what he calls a "time bomb": the need to invest in new voting technology, particularly to replace aging voting machines. "There has been a terrible market failure in voting technology which needs to be addressed," he writes, "(and which needs federal funding—something the commissioners don't call for)." This is also a partisan issue. In an environment like the one in which we find ourselves, imagine the urgency with which Republican members of Congress will seek to allocate more federal money to make voting easier. Primary opponents' attack ads practically write themselves.

The real problem on Election Day is that the people who run elections are the same ones that rely on their outcome. That is the first fix that's needed to encourage more voting, and the one that is probably hardest to implement.

> *"Policies that would make our ballots less accessible to Americans based on what language they speak would be at odds with that historical arc towards expanding the franchise."*

Bilingual Ballots Protect Voting Rights

Adam Serwer

Adam Serwer is a former reporter at Mother Jones *and a reporter at* MSNBC. *In the following viewpoint, he reports that Republican presidential candidates Mitt Romney and Newt Gingrich came out in support of English-language-only ballots. Serwer says this would be in violation of the Voting Rights Act, which provides for bilingual ballots. Republicans want to appeal to Hispanics, Serwer says, but at the same time, Republicans are trying to appeal to voters who resent Spanish speakers. Especially in Florida, Serwer says, this is a difficult line to walk.*

As you read, consider the following questions:

1. According to Serwer, what was the George W. Bush administration's record like in terms of bilingual ballots?

Adam Serwer, "Gingrich and Romney Want to Say Adios to Bilingual Ballots," *Mother Jones*, January 30, 2012. Copyright © 2012 by Foundation for National Progress. All rights reserved. Reproduced by permission.

2. How does the Voting Rights Act affect the issue of bilingual ballots specifically?

3. Why might Republicans be willing to have only English ballots in Florida, even though many voters there are ethnic Cubans?

As Republican primary voters head to the polls in Florida on Tuesday [2012], both GOP front-runners have endorsed a policy that would contradict existing law and could disenfranchise millions of voters across the country.

Republicans Against Spanish

During a recent debate, both Newt Gingrich and Mitt Romney supported getting rid of bilingual ballots when the topic was brought up by the moderator. "I would have ballots in English," Gingrich said. "And I think you could have programs where virtually everybody would be able to read the ballots." Romney agreed. "I think Speaker Gingrich is right with regards to what he's described," he said.

That wasn't much of a stretch for Gingrich, who once called Spanish "the language of living in a ghetto." Yet their glib demand for English-only ballots would require amending the Voting Rights Act and doing away with hard-won legal requirements that have existed for decades. It's a sharp turn away from the [George W.] Bush administration, which despite a spotty civil rights record filed more ballot access cases on behalf of non-English speakers than any administration had before.

"We used to have poll taxes, we used to have whites-only primaries, we used to not let women vote," says Myrna Pérez, senior counsel with the Brennan Center [for Justice's] Democracy Program. "Policies that would make our ballots less accessible to Americans based on what language they speak would be at odds with that historical arc towards expanding the franchise."

Bilingual ballots are no abstract issue in Florida, which has a sizeable population of Americans whose first languages are Spanish or Haitian Creole. "The Haitian population is a voting bloc, the Hispanic community is a voting bloc," says Carolyn Thompson, a Florida-based activist with the Advancement Project, a civil rights group. "They pay taxes, they've won the right to vote in their language."

Under the 1975 revision of the Voting Rights Act, communities whose non-English-speaking populations reach a certain level have to provide voting materials in alternate languages.

There are 238 jurisdictions covered by the Voting Rights Act's language requirements. It's hard to tell how many voters would be impacted by the repeal of those provisions, but the census estimates that there are more than 19 million eligible voters who come from the communities the law is meant to serve. Ten counties in Florida are among them, four of which went Republican in the last presidential election.

"Some of these ballot measures involve very complex legal language," Camila Gallardo of the Latino civil rights organization National Council of La Raza points out. "Some of the language is hard to understand even for fluent English speakers, let alone if your first language isn't English."

Hispanic Voters

Republicans have long had a complex relationship with Florida. It's the site of great conservative victories, like George W. Bush seizing the presidency in 2000 and Marco Rubio crushing his challengers in 2010's Senate race. But it's also the kind of place where moderates like Jeb Bush and Charlie Crist thrive, a cosmopolitan state that anti-immigrant ex-GOP congressman Tom Tancredo once compared to the Tower of Babel. That's why Gingrich followed up Monday's debate with an appearance on the Spanish-language station Univision in which he called Romney's draconian approach to curtailing illegal immigration an "Obama-level fantasy," and why Romney

Mandating Bilingual Ballots

Imagine that you are a registered voter and want to exercise your fundamental right to participate in the political process. You have trouble locating your designated polling site because you cannot read either the written instructions that accompanied your voter registration card or the posted signs directing you to the site. If you are fortunate enough to arrive at the correct destination, you encounter poll workers who are speaking incomprehensible words and are visibly irritated when you do not know how to respond to them. When you give them your name, the poll workers cannot find it in their registration books. Even if they find your name and give you a ballot, you do not know what to do with it. A look of embarrassment spreads across your face.... You cannot read the ballot that is given to you. Alone and without any guidance, you attempt to cast a meaningful ballot.

The language assistance provisions of the Voting Rights Act (VRA) were enacted to remove language barriers to voting. A permanent requirement for bilingual voting materials and assistance was included in the original 1965 act, but was limited to only Puerto Rican voters who were educated in Spanish. In 1975, Congress added a temporary mandate that included Alaska Natives, American Indians, Asian Americans, and persons of Spanish heritage who had suffered from educational discrimination. That mandate, contained in Sections 4(f)(4) and 203, prohibits jurisdictions with prescribed levels of limited-English proficient (LEP) voting-age U.S. citizens from conducting English-only elections....

James Thomas Tucker, The Battle over Bilingual Ballots:
Language Minorities and Political Access Under the
Voting Rights Act. *Burlington, VT: Ashgate Publishing, 2009.*

turned Gingrich's remarks about Spanish being "ghetto" into a campaign ad. In Florida, a Republican who comes off as anti-immigrant or anti-Hispanic could see their political ambitions cut short fast. It's a difficult balancing act for members of a party that is seen as increasingly hostile by Latino voters, who are becoming more influential in American elections.

"They try to appeal to Latinos and Florida and during the general election, but everywhere else they're trying to be tough guys," says Dr. Gary Segura of the national polling firm Latino Decisions. "It's going to be very difficult for them to have it both ways."

More than 1 out of 10 Republican primary voters is Latino in Florida, so it's possible that Romney and Gingrich's commitment to English primacy, if applied, could disenfranchise part of their own base in the state. Or they could just be banking on the possibility that their voters are more likely to be completely bilingual.

"The Cuban population heavily concentrated in the Republican Party are bilingual, fluent, are likely to be able to hang with that," says Segura. "Some number of Republicans would be disenfranchised, but the largest number would be first-generation Puerto Rican Democrats."

Changing federal law isn't easy of course, and the Voting Rights Act was renewed in 2006 for another 25 years. By the time it's up for consideration again, Republicans might have even less interest in ensuring that language minorities have equal access to the ballot box, even in Florida.

"For a long time, Cubans were staunchly in the Republican column, although that demographic is really changing," says Gallardo. "[Today] you see a lot of young Hispanics registering with no party affiliation."

| "A perverse element of the Voting Rights Act makes the whole scheme possible, and, unfortunately, not even Republicans have been willing to challenge it."

Bilingual Ballots Are Unnecessary and Can Lead to Fraud

Linda Chavez

Linda Chavez is a radio talk show host, Fox News analyst, syndicated columnist, and the author of An Unlikely Conservative: The Transformation of an Ex-Liberal. *In the following viewpoint, she says that virtually all US citizens speak English and that federal law overstates the number of Americans who cannot read ballots. She argues that allowing bilingual ballots is an unnecessary expense and makes it possible for undocumented immigrants to vote illegally. She also says bilingual ballots undermine the unity of American identity. She says that the Voting Rights Act provisions for bilingual ballots should be repealed.*

As you read, consider the following questions:

1. According to Chavez, why is English proficiency rarely a problem among naturalized citizens?

2. What action does Chavez say tripled the number of jurisdictions forced to provide bilingual ballots?

3. What does "E pluribus unum" mean, and why does Chavez feel the motto is important to the debate on bilingual ballots?

At a time when many state and local governments cannot afford even necessary government programs, the [Barack] Obama administration is about to force hundreds of jurisdictions to waste millions of dollars printing ballots in Spanish and other languages for voters who don't need them. Worse, some of these bilingual ballots may be used fraudulently to encourage people who are not citizens to vote illegally in next year's [2012's] election.

Unnecessary Expense

A perverse element of the Voting Rights Act makes the whole scheme possible, and, unfortunately, not even Republicans have been willing to challenge it.

Under the act, jurisdictions whose population includes at least 5 percent of voting-age citizens who have limited English proficiency must provide ballots and other voting materials in other languages. Currently, about 500 jurisdictions are required to do so.

I have repeatedly testified before Congress against this provision. As I have argued, there are exceedingly few persons who are actually eligible to vote who can't understand English. English proficiency among U.S.-born Hispanics is virtually universal. And even among naturalized citizens, English proficiency is rarely a problem, since demonstrating English proficiency is required to become a U.S. citizen.

So how is it that so many jurisdictions end up having to provide materials in Spanish, Chinese and other languages, when so few eligible voters really need them?

It has to do with the way the government determines who is English-proficient and who isn't.

The Census Bureau, which is charged under the Voting Rights Act with determining which jurisdictions will be required to print bilingual voting materials, uses a remarkably dubious methodology to determine how many citizens are not proficient in English. Since 1982, the bureau on its census forms has counted those who are members of so-called language minorities and who say they speak English "well" as having limited proficiency. Doing so in 1982 tripled the number of jurisdictions forced to provide bilingual ballots.

In many places, these bilingual materials just sit unused during elections—a waste of money that could be spent elsewhere. A 1997 General Accounting Office [(GAO), presently known as the Government Accountability Office] report noted that the printing of bilingual material accounted for half the election costs in those jurisdictions covered. And an earlier GAO study found that in most jurisdictions required to print bilingual materials, not a single person requested them. Could there be a more egregious waste of public funds?

Noncitizens Voting

But the greater danger is that unscrupulous groups sometimes use these materials to facilitate voting by noncitizens. As I have testified, multiple instances of voter fraud have involved noncitizens voting—by using bilingual ballots—from Hawaii to Georgia.

So what can be done? The best thing would be to repeal the onerous provision—but not even a Republican-controlled Congress has been willing to take on that fight. Short of repeal, the very least that should be done is stopping the Census Bureau from inflating the number of jurisdictions required to provide bilingual materials based on phony limited-English-proficient numbers.

The current chairmen of the House subcommittees charged with overseeing enforcement of the Voting Rights Act's bilingual provisions have asked the assistant attorney general for civil rights and the head of the bureau to abandon the flawed methodology now being used. In a letter this week, Reps. Trent Franks and Trey Gowdy urged the bureau to adopt the commonsense approach of considering anyone who says they speak English "well" on the census form as English-proficient.

At least this standard would result in fewer unnecessary bilingual ballots from being printed. But the only way to stop this nonsense is to eliminate the requirement for bilingual voting materials altogether. Furthermore, there is another reason to oppose them: they balkanize our nation.

Our original national motto is "E pluribus unum"—out of many, one. While we come from all over the globe, we are united as Americans. This unity means that we hold certain things in common. We celebrate the same democratic values, cherish our many freedoms, and champion equality under the law. Our common bonds must also include an ability to communicate with one another through a common language: English.

In our struggling economy, there is no better time than now to stop wasting money on bilingual ballots.

"Instead of a community deliberation culminating in a shared day of decision, an election like the one here is diffuse and inferior."

The Stakes of Florida's Special Election

George F. Will

George F. Will is a newspaper columnist and an author. In the following viewpoint, he reports on a special election in Florida that is a close contest and one that he says will indicate that Democrats are in trouble nationally if the Republican candidate wins. He says that the Republican candidate is hobbled by not having sufficient money. Early voting means that many voters will cast ballots before the Republican candidate can get his message out, Will argues. He concludes that early voting distorts elections and should be abolished.

As you read, consider the following questions:

1. Why does Will say that the axiom "all politics is local" has been invalidated?

2. What is the breakdown of Democrats and Republicans in the special election district, according to Will?

3. Who gets an absentee ballot automatically in Florida, according to Will?

Because it is this year's first federal election, attention must be paid to the March 11 [2014] voting to fill a Florida congressional seat vacated by the death in October of Republican C.W. Bill Young, who served in Congress for 43 years. If Democrat Alex Sink wins, the significance will be minimal because she enjoys multiple advantages. Hence if Republican David Jolly prevails, Republicans will construe this as evidence that Barack Obama has become an anvil in the saddle of every Democratic candidate.

Special Election

Matters are, however, murky. [Former House Speaker] Tip O'Neill's axiom that "all politics is local" has been rendered anachronistic by the national government that liberals such as O'Neill created. Today's administrative state touches everyone everywhere, so all politics is partly national. Politics in Florida's 13th Congressional District today concerns the National Flood Insurance Program (NFIP).

Obama carried this Gulf Coast district, a one-county constituency near Tampa, by 3.8 points in 2008 and 1.4 points in 2012. Although Sink hadn't lived in the district until very recently, she has almost 100 percent name recognition here because she has run statewide, almost winning the governorship in 2010, when she carried the county by 5.7 points. Between 2007 and 2011, she was Florida's chief financial officer.

After Young died, the national and state Democratic parties moved with more dispatch than seemliness. With a robust disregard for traditional niceties, they moved Sink into the 13th District. Her real home in another county is, Jolly says—he exaggerates—closer to Disney World than to this

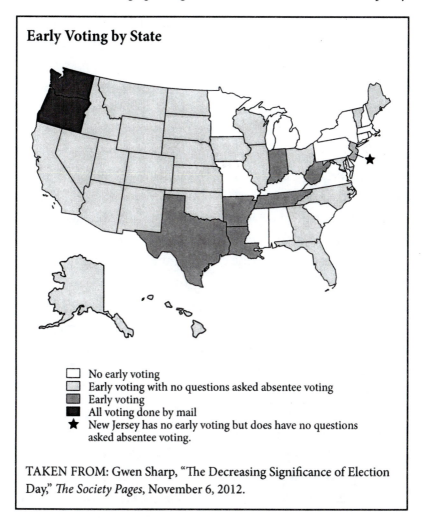

Early Voting by State

☐ No early voting
☐ Early voting with no questions asked absentee voting
▨ Early voting
■ All voting done by mail
★ New Jersey has no early voting but does have no questions
   asked absentee voting.

TAKEN FROM: Gwen Sharp, "The Decreasing Significance of Election
Day," *The Society Pages*, November 6, 2012.

district's beaches. They also prevented a primary challenge
from anyone who really lives here, thereby allowing Jolly to
say that national Democrats decided no local Democrat was
qualified to represent the locals.

While Sink rented an apartment and began raising money,
Jolly fought a nine-week primary race, from which he emerged
on Jan. 14 financially depleted. He worked for Young for many
years, which helps his résumé, but then became a Washington
lobbyist, which does not. He thinks it should, saying mor-

dantly that politics "is the one industry in which experience and qualifications count against you." He notes that whoever wins next month will have to run again in November and, if he is running then, the Republican House leadership will want to give him some plums beneficial to his district—perhaps assignment to committees to protect seniors and veterans.

This is a purple but not a polarized district, with 37 percent Republican and 35 percent Democrat. Although the district gave the world the first Hooters restaurant, the district is unusually elderly, white and disapproving of Obamacare [referring to the Patient Protection and Affordable Care Act]. It also is smoldering about the flood insurance program.

The NFIP is yet another entitlement program that is proving to be more durable, and more emblematic of modern America, than Mount Rushmore. The federal government has long subsidized insurance for homeowners who live in coastal areas or flood plains. This entitlement, covering about 5.5 million of America's 122 million housing units, is necessary because otherwise people would be required to pay the costs of the risks they choose to run for living where they are pleased to live. The NFIP enables the disproportionately wealthy people who own beach properties to socialize their storm losses while keeping private the pleasures of their real estate. The NFIP is another illustration of the entitlement state's upward distribution of benefits.

Recent attempts to reform the NFIP—to end subsidized rates for 1.1 million properties and to change rates based on improved risk assessments—threaten to raise by thousands of dollars the annual insurance costs of some property owners here. Both Sink and Jolly are competitively indignant. But the Senate, an unsleeping defender of entitlements benefiting the privileged (witness the new farm bill), has recently derailed reform.

The Evils of Early Voting

Sink will benefit from the national trend allowing early voting to obliterate Election Day. Any Floridian who has ever requested an absentee ballot henceforth gets one automatically. Seventy-seven percent of the Republican primary votes here were cast by mail in the Jan. 14 primary, and absentee ballots will be mailed Feb. 7. Furthermore, early voting at polling places begins March 1, so many—perhaps most—votes will be cast before Jolly has raised much of the money necessary to communicate his message.

Instead of a community deliberation culminating in a shared day of decision, an election like the one here is diffuse and inferior. If Sink wins, Republicans nationally can shrug; if Jolly wins, Democrats should tremble. But no matter who wins, the district loses because it has lost Election Day.

> "We haven't seen a period of constrict-
> ing the franchise like this since Jim
> Crow."

Restrictions on Early Voting Are Discriminatory

Dan Froomkin

Dan Froomkin is the senior Washington correspondent for the Huffington Post. In the following viewpoint, he reports that early voting had been introduced in many states, including Ohio, as a way to end long lines at the polls. It had been very success-ful in getting more people to the polls, especially minority voters. However, Froomkin says, its success concerns Republicans, who worry that minority voters cast most of their ballots for Demo-crats. Republicans have therefore worked to restrict early voting, especially in urban minority communities. Froomkin argues that these restrictions are discriminatory and un-American.

As you read, consider the following questions:

1. Why were members of Cleveland's Greater Abyssinia Baptist Church able to vote after services in 2008, ac-cording to Froomkin?

2. What percentage of early in-person voting was made up of black voters in 2008 in Ohio, and how does that compare to those who voted on Election Day or by mail?

3. What claim by Mitt Romney did the *New York Times* term "an extraordinary lie," according to the viewpoint?

Washington—Four years ago, on the Sunday before Election Day 2008, members of predominantly African American congregations in Cleveland went straight from celebrating God to rejoicing in their right to vote.

Too Successful

"We had buses at every church that Sunday," recalled the Rev. Emmitt Theophilus Caviness, the 83-year-old pastor of Cleveland's Greater Abyssinia Baptist Church. "As soon as we left church, we got on the bus and went down to vote."

At the board of elections office, Caviness told *HuffPost*, "you would have seen long lines, wrapped around corners. People were enthusiastic. They were having fun."

It was a first in so many ways. But one of the most important of those ways was the new Ohio law that allowed voting on a Sunday. "It never would have happened had we not had early voting—the opportunity on the last weekend to participate in democracy," Caviness said.

Four years earlier, the November election in Ohio was a debacle. Shortages of voting machines in some minority neighborhoods led to thousands of voters giving up their franchise rather than waiting for as long as 10 hours for their turn. Other votes went uncounted.

In response, Ohio's legislature established early in-person voting, supplementing traditional Election Day voting and mail-in absentee ballots. Voters would now have 35 days before the election to cast ballots, including that final weekend.

In 2008, some 93,000 Ohioans—including the members of the Greater Abyssinia Baptist Church—cast votes during those last three days before the election.

But early voting was apparently too much of a success for some people. In Ohio and four other states—Florida, Georgia, Tennessee and West Virginia—Republican-led legislatures have dramatically reduced early voting in 2012 as part of what can only be explained as a concerted effort to suppress the votes of Democratic-leaning voters. Other parts of that effort include voter ID [identification] bills, intimidation of voter registration groups and the purges of voter rolls.

In Ohio and Florida, two of the most critical swing states in this year's presidential election, the GOP early voting rollback specifically included a ban on voting on the Sunday before Election Day.

Early voting started off a wildly popular, bipartisan element of voting reform. Indeed, of all the voting reforms this country has seen over the last decades, early voting is easily the most unassailable. It makes voting more convenient for the public and makes Election Day easier for election officials. Because it generally happens at board of elections offices, it takes notoriously unreliable volunteer poll workers out of the picture.

But Republican leaders cooled on the idea after 2008. "It just so happened that this was the first time that early voting had been used in large numbers to mobilize African American and Latino voters," said Wendy Weiser, who directs the Democracy Program at the Brennan Center for Justice at New York University School of Law.

After the GOP won control of many statehouses in 2010, rolling back early voting became a top legislative priority. That meant reducing the period for early in-person voting in Florida from 14 to 8 days, and in Ohio, from 35 to 11. And no voting on Sunday before the election.

The First Early Voting

Texas, the first state to establish early voting, began its program gradually. In 1987 the state legislature passed a measure eliminating the requirement that individuals voting absentee must state a reason for doing so. Absentee voting had come to be known as the liar's ballot because the reasons given often were considered simply excuses for being permitted to vote early by mail. In 1989 the state legislature enacted legislation that required the most populous counties to offer extended voting hours for the final week of absentee voting. In 1991 the legislature took the final step toward early voting, allowing any eligible voter to cast an early ballot during a period generally beginning 17 days before the election and ending on the fourth day before the election at designated locations. Those who are away from their county on election day or during early voting, who are sick or disabled, who are at least 65 years of age, who are confined to jail but still eligible to vote, or who are in the military and previously resided in Texas may vote early by mail.

Glenn H. Utter and Ruth Ann Strickland,
Campaign and Election Reform: A Reference Handbook.
Santa Barbara, CA: ABC-CLIO, 2008.

Partisan Motives

"I try to be an objective observer," said professor Paul Gronke, who runs the nonpartisan Early Voting Information Center at Reed College in Oregon. "But the objective facts indicate there seem to be partisan motivations behind the ratcheting back of early in-person voting."

Research by an Ohio voter advocacy group found that blacks made up more than half the early in-person voters in 2008, compared with about a quarter of people who vote on Election Day or by mail.

Research by political scientists at Dartmouth College and the University of Florida concluded that "Democratic, African American, Hispanic, younger, and first-time voters were disproportionately likely to vote early in 2008 and in particular on weekends, including the final Sunday of early voting."

"We should be increasing access to vote, not taking it away," said Ohio state Sen. Nina Turner, a Cleveland Democrat. "You got a lot of working people, working-class folks, some people have to piece together three to four jobs, why wouldn't we have extended hours and extended days?"

The question ultimately answers itself. "For me, this is Jim Crow in the 21st century," Turner said. "Jim Crow has been resurrected. This is by design. It's not by accident."

Republican explanations for rolling back early voting include unsupported suggestions of voter fraud. Ohio secretary of state Jon Husted, a Republican, said in a newspaper op-ed that his goal "has been to balance access and accuracy," and that he was simply trying to establish "a uniform system across the state" with the early voting rules.

But Pastor Caviness said he thinks Republicans were intimidated by seeing all those African-American churchgoers headed to vote—"Souls to Polls" is what the black churches called it. "That seems to be the tenor and tune of where they're coming from," Caviness said. "Otherwise, why would you deny people the basic right to participate in democracy?"

In Ohio's heavily Democratic cities—Cleveland, Columbus, Akron and Toledo—early voting will be limited to working hours on weekdays in 2012. But, as the *Cincinnati Enquirer* reported recently, attempts to add extended hours at the local election boards have been blocked by Republicans in urban counties "even as extended hours will be available in some smaller counties with a strong Republican slant."

The reason, as Ari Berman explained in the *Nation*, is that county boards of election in Ohio have two members from each party. Ties are broken by the secretary of state.

In solidly Republican counties, GOP election commissioners have approved expanded early voting hours—because why not? But in Democratic counties, they've balked. And Husted, the man who said he supports the law because it will bring uniformity to the state, has backed them up.

The early voting changes in both Florida and Ohio face legal challenges. Rep. Corrine Brown (D-Fla.) has filed a federal lawsuit seeking to block the reduction, which she argued is discriminatory.

And President Barack Obama's campaign sued Husted last month, asking a federal court to restore voting during the last three days before the election on the grounds that the law grants unequal treatment to military families, who are allowed later polling access than other Ohio voters.

Un-American

The Romney campaign tried to cast Obama's action as an attack on military voting rights. That claim, which a member of the *New York Times* editorial board termed "an extraordinary lie"—was initially accepted stenographically by some political journalists, and spread like wildfire on social networks, before crumbling under the weight of its own mendacity.

Matt McClellan, Husted's press secretary, denied there was any partisan motivation behind the restriction in early voting. "The boards of election had requested that to have more opportunity to prepare for Election Day," McClellan told the *Huffington Post*. The Ohio Association of Election Officials "asked for it."

But Llyn McCoy, president of the election officials' group, disagreed: "I wouldn't say that we came out and started this," she said.

The election officials' group was asked to weigh in on the idea, McCoy said—and it did end up voting in favor of reducing early voting days. But it was hardly unanimous. "It was a close vote," she said.

The biggest split was between officials from rural counties, who didn't feel the need for extended hours, and those from urban counties, who felt it strongly.

McCoy, deputy director of the board of elections in Greene County, a mostly Republican county outside Dayton, was nevertheless among the officials who argued in favor of voting during that final weekend.

"By and large, election officials, it's our job to make it easier for people to vote, not harder," she said. "That's where a lot of us came down."

People who follow the history of voting rights are amazed at the sudden turnaround in what had seemed irreversible momentum toward greater access to the ballot.

"We haven't seen a period of constricting the franchise like this since Jim Crow," Weiser said. "It really runs contrary to the American narrative."

Turner, the state senator from Cleveland, called it "pure racism."

"It's racist, it's sexist and it's classist," Turner said. "It's just flat-out un-American."

"*[Ranked-choice voting] contributes to improving our democracy in certain respects but still falls short of its promise to improve participation by all parts of our community.*"

Ranked-Choice Voting in Minneapolis Has Contributed to Inequality

Lawrence R. Jacobs and Joanne M. Miller

Lawrence R. Jacobs is director of the Center for the Study of Politics and Governance at the University of Minnesota's Humphrey School of Public Affairs. Joanne M. Miller is an associate professor in the university's Department of Political Science. In the following viewpoint, they discuss the use of ranked-choice voting (RCV) in Minneapolis. RCV allows voters to rank three candidates by preference. The authors say this has reduced negative campaigning, since candidates do not want to alienate the opposition and lose the chance of being ranked as a second or third choice. However, promises that voting results are more equitable under RCV are undercut, the authors say, by the fact that those in minority and poorer communities have more trouble filling out the complicated ballots.

As you read, consider the following questions:

1. According to the viewpoint, what did FairVote Minnesota promise about RCV and equality?

2. What do the authors say about the turnout gap in RCV elections in Minneapolis?

3. What role do candidates have in improving elections under RCV, according to the authors?

Ranked-choice voting—the grand experiment in elections that Minneapolis tried out again last fall—may salve some of what ails our democracy. But, for now, it leaves open the well-documented voting gap that favors white voters and the affluent. That populist conclusion arises from careful statistical analyses of votes in the Minneapolis election and the evidence it yields of differences in participation between communities of color and the poor vs. their white and affluent counterparts.

RCV Successes and Failures

We take our hats off to the enthusiasts of ranked-choice voting (or RCV) for sizing up problems in our democracy and then rolling up their sleeves to do the hard work of actually reforming elections in Minneapolis. We also salute another accomplishment: The RCV process—in which voters rank up to three preferred candidates, and then the weakest vote-getters are dropped until one of those remaining achieves a majority—accomplished something that truly astounds us. Negative campaigning became bad politics.

Slamming an opponent risked alienating his or her supporters and losing any chance of securing their second- or third-place rankings. Here's something we've never seen: The media and voters struggled to detect candidate criticisms of one another during the Minneapolis mayor's election. Did

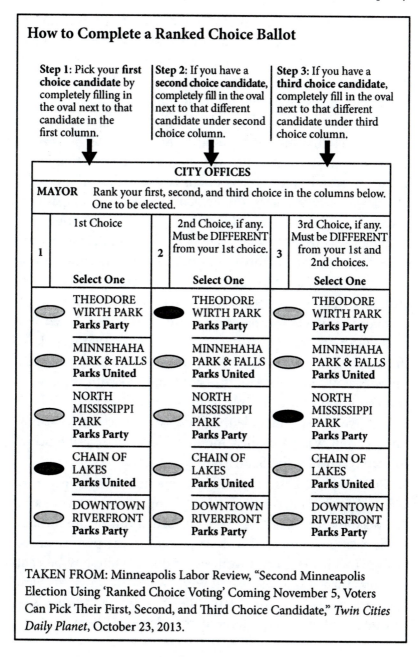

How to Complete a Ranked Choice Ballot

Step 1: Pick your **first choice candidate** by completely filling in the oval next to that candidate in the first column.

Step 2: If you have a **second choice candidate**, completely fill in the oval next to that different candidate under second choice column.

Step 3: If you have a **third choice candidate**, completely fill in the oval next to that different candidate under third choice column.

CITY OFFICES

MAYOR   Rank your first, second, and third choice in the columns below. One to be elected.

	1st Choice		2nd Choice, if any. Must be DIFFERENT from your 1st choice.		3rd Choice, if any. Must be DIFFERENT from your 1st and 2nd choices.
1	**Select One**	**2**	**Select One**	**3**	**Select One**
⬭	THEODORE WIRTH PARK **Parks Party**	⬤	THEODORE WIRTH PARK **Parks Party**	⬭	THEODORE WIRTH PARK **Parks Party**
⬭	MINNEHAHA PARK & FALLS **Parks United**	⬭	MINNEHAHA PARK & FALLS **Parks United**	⬭	MINNEHAHA PARK & FALLS **Parks United**
⬭	NORTH MISSISSIPPI PARK **Parks Party**	⬭	NORTH MISSISSIPPI PARK **Parks Party**	⬤	NORTH MISSISSIPPI PARK **Parks Party**
⬤	CHAIN OF LAKES **Parks United**	⬭	CHAIN OF LAKES **Parks United**	⬭	CHAIN OF LAKES **Parks United**
⬭	DOWNTOWN RIVERFRONT **Parks Party**	⬭	DOWNTOWN RIVERFRONT **Parks Party**	⬭	DOWNTOWN RIVERFRONT **Parks Party**

TAKEN FROM: Minneapolis Labor Review, "Second Minneapolis Election Using 'Ranked Choice Voting' Coming November 5, Voters Can Pick Their First, Second, and Third Choice Candidate," *Twin Cities Daily Planet*, October 23, 2013.

anyone following the 2012 presidential election struggle to identify [Democrat] Barack Obama's and [Republican] Mitt Romney's differences?

But fans of RCV promised more. FairVote Minnesota, its champion, announced in its 2013 press kit that the reform ensures that a "larger, more diverse swath of the electorate gets to participate in the political process." Important promise—equal voice for each citizen is a fundamental democratic principle. What does the evidence show?

We carefully examined voting in the 13 wards in Minneapolis to see if RCV contributed to broader participation based on actual vote returns obtained from the Minneapolis city clerk. Unfortunately, the evidence shows a clear pattern. Voters who were more affluent and white turned out at a higher rate, completed their ballots more accurately and were more likely to use all three opportunities to rank their most preferred candidates compared with voters living in low-income neighborhoods and in communities of color.

Specifically, we compared the three wards that stood out as the most affluent (11, 12 and 13) with those that were least affluent (2, 3, and 5), as well as those that had the highest percentage of white voters (10, 11, 12 and 13) with those with greatest proportion of people from communities of color (4, 5 and 9). We did not include the Sixth Ward, because its voting participation was an outlier; the disparities we describe below are stronger when the Sixth Ward is included.

RCV did not close the well-documented turnout gap that favors affluent and white voters. Among registered voters in the most affluent wards, 42 percent turned out in the Minneapolis election, compared with 28 percent in the poorest areas. In wards with the greatest concentration of whites, 39 percent of voters turned out, compared with 26 percent in wards with the most people of color. These differences are statistically significant, justifying a high level of confidence in them.

Complicated Ballot

The complicated RCV ballot—including its new rules and rows of candidates—raised another obstacle. In economically better off sections of town, 3.36 percent of the ballots were "spoiled"—the legal term for voter stumbles in selecting candidates according to strict guidelines—compared with 4.92 percent in the poorer parts. The comparable proportions for communities with smaller and larger proportions of racial minorities were 3.37 percent and 5.77 percent, respectively. These differences are highly significant in statistical terms.

Advocates for RCV also champion its pioneering process for recording a fuller range of voter preferences by allowing citizens to rank up to three candidates. Unfortunately, the better-off were advantaged here, too. In affluent wards, 21 percent of voters failed to fill out all three preferences, compared with 24 percent in poorer neighborhoods. The comparable proportions for white and minority wards were 22 percent and 26 percent, respectively. Although these differences may appear small, they are highly significant in statistical terms, indicating a robust and important pattern.

How important are these results? Racial and income disparities in Minneapolis triggered public alarm when they produced one of the largest "education gaps" in the country. What we are pointing to represents another disparity—a "democracy gap."

Passions run hot on RCV. Our research is not an "interpretation" or "opinion." It is a sober, objective analysis of voting results from the Minneapolis city clerk's data.

Let's turn down the passion around RCV and put on our thinking caps. RCV contributes to improving our democracy in certain respects but still falls short of its promise to improve participation by all parts of our community.

What can be done? Plans to decrease the number of candidates and possibly revise the ballot to reduce its complexity might help. We also would recommend new thought about how the city and media can improve the quality of information that is distributed to all communities.

Candidates have a role, too. Playing hide-and-seek on differences to avoid alienating opponents' supporters deliberately trips up voters who are trying to accurately sort the campaigns. We need to set expectations and scrutinize candidates to come clean on where they stand and how they differ from their rivals.

> "*[Ranked-choice voting] cannot fix these structural inequalities, but it certainly did not cause them.*"

Ranked-Choice Voting in Minneapolis Has Not Contributed to Inequality

David Schultz

David Schultz is Hamline University professor of political science and author of Election Law and Democratic Theory *and* American Politics in the Age of Ignorance: Why Lawmakers Choose Belief over Research. *In the following viewpoint, he argues that ranked-choice voting (RCV), in which voters can select their choice for a first, second, and third candidate, has nothing to do with racial or class inequalities in voting. Rather, he says, racial and class inequalities are ingrained in the American system and are endemic in non-RCV voting. RCV was not meant to solve all of the problems with American inequality, he says, and it is not surprising that it has not. He argues that this is no reason to reject RCV.*

As you read, consider the following questions:

1. What evidence does Schultz provide that maldistributions in wealth are growing?

David Schultz, "Race, Class and RCV: Why the Jacobs-Miller Study Is Largely Irrelevant," *MinnPost*, February 17, 2014. Copyright © 2014 by MinnPost. All rights reserved. Reproduced by permission.

2. According to Schultz, evidence suggests that America remains as racially divided today as in the time of what court case?

3. What baseline does Schultz say Jacobs and Miller should have used to assess the success of RCV?

Race and class structurally divide the United States. Economically we live in two nations separate but unequal, with political power and privilege fractured along this divide. Thus it comes as no surprise that professors Larry Jacobs and Joanne Miller recently found that the use of ranked-choice voting (RCV) by voters in the 2013 Minneapolis elections largely tracked this class and racial divide. Conceding that their statistics are largely correct, their analysis and conclusions are largely irrelevant to the debate about RCV, voting, or political power in Minneapolis or the United States.

First, there is no debate that race and class divide America. A 2011 Congressional Budget Office study found that the after-tax income gap (after calculating in transfer payments and welfare) between the top 1 percent of the population and everyone else more than tripled since 1979. Between 1973 and 2007, after-tax income for the top 1 percent increased by 275 percent. For the bottom quintile it was merely 18 percent, while for middle class or middle three quintiles it increased by not quite 40 percent. According to the Census Bureau, the median family income fell in 2012 from $51,100 to $51,017, with average Americans earning less now than they did in real dollars in 1989. However, there is some good news. Since 2009, the income of the wealthiest 1 percent has increased by 31 percent.

Wealth Also Tells the Story

But income only tells part of the story. Maldistributions in wealth are exacerbated and growing. According to the Institute for Policy Studies, the top 1 percent controls almost 34 percent of the wealth in the country, with half of the population possessing less than 3 percent in 2007. The racial disparities for wealth mirror those of income. Since 2007 the wealth gap has increased as the value of American homes—the single largest source of wealth for most Americans—has eroded. Studies such as the Survey of Consumer Finances by the Federal Reserve Board have similarly concluded that the wealth gap has increased since the 1980s.

According to an April 2013 Pew Research Center report titled "A Rise in Wealth for the Wealthy; Declines for the Lower 93%," since the crash of 2008, the "mean net worth of households in the upper 7% of the wealth distribution rose by an estimated 28%, while the mean net worth of households in the lower 93% dropped by 4%." The richest have recovered nicely from the Great Recession, the rest of us have not done so well. Moreover, the income gap has a racial component. A recent Census Bureau report stated that in 2012 the median household income for whites was $57,009, for Hispanics it was $39,005 and for blacks $33,321.

The wealth disparities across race were even worse. A policy brief from Brandeis University's Institute on Assets and Social Policy found that over the past 25 years, the wealth gap between African-Americans and whites tripled from $85,000 in 1984 to $236,500 in 2009. For the few African-Americans and whites at the same income level, the latter had wealth at least three if not more times that of the former.

No Change Since *Brown*

Repeatedly, the evidence suggests that we remain as racially divided today as we were 60 years ago when the Supreme Court's *Brown v. Board of Education* decision supposedly de-segregated America's schools and launched a civil rights revolution. Books such as *American Apartheid*, by Douglas Massey and Nancy Denton, and *Poverty and Place: Ghettos, Barrios, and the American City*, by Paul Jargowsky, document the racial segregation of contemporary America, and Andrew Hacker's *Two Nations: Black and White, Separate, Hostile, Unequal* describes the contrasting social worlds of America. Closer to home, it was 20 years ago while I was working with John A. Powell at the University of Minnesota's Institute on Race and Poverty that we documented Minneapolis as one of the three most racially segregated cities in America. . . .

No voting system, whether it be RCV or the old one that it replaced in Minneapolis, is going to rectify or mitigate the racial-class inequities that already exist in this country. To conclude as Jacobs and Miller did that RCV "leaves open the well-documented voting gap" and reveals "differences in participation between communities of color and the poor vs. their white and affluent counterparts" (quoting from their Feb. 12 *Star Tribune* commentary) largely misses the point. That voting gap existed before the implementation of RCV and there is no indication that the system it replaced did anything to ameliorate the gap.

Their study seems to imply that RCV caused the voting gap or that RCV was supposed to address the voting gap but didn't. Jacobs and Miller deserve credit for pointing out that there is a class and racial gap in voting in Minneapolis, but that is nothing new or novel. Nor is their argument that more education is necessary to teach people how to use RCV. I as much said that four years ago in the initial study of RCV in Minneapolis.

Finally, the Jacobs-Miller study uses the wrong baseline for assessing RCV. They point to the low participation rates among the poor and people of color in the 2013 Minneapolis elections as a flaw with RCV. But compared to what, the turnout in other general elections or in primaries? If we compare to primaries, the turnout was much greater, whereas with the former a small band of white affluents or party insiders dominated the selection process. If we compare to other general elections, then it is not so clear that their results are statistically significant, especially based on one election.

RCV is not a panacea for all that ails American democracy. The core issue is how class, race, and to some extent gender, allocate political power and influence in the United States. RCV cannot fix these structural inequalities, but it certainly did not cause them—as the Jacobs and Miller study seems to imply.

Periodical and Internet Sources Bibliography

The following articles have been selected to supplement the diverse views presented in this chapter.

Josh Israel	"MSNBC Host Grills Ohio Secretary of State for Cutting Early Voting," *ThinkProgress* (blog), May 8, 2014.
Lawrence R. Jacobs and Joanne M. Miller	"Ranked-Choice Voting: By the Data, Still Flawed," *Star Tribune* (Minneapolis, MN), February 12, 2014.
Tim Penny and David Durenberger	"We Need Ranked-Choice Voting at the National Level," MinnPost, October 21, 2013.
Rob Richie	"Overseas Voters from 5 States to Use Ranked Choice Voting Ballots in 2014 Congressional Election," *Huffington Post*, April 17, 2014.
Rob Richie and Devin McCarthy	"A Ranked-Choice Voting System for Congress," *Washington Post*, October 17, 2013.
Zachary Roth	"Ohio Cuts Early Voting Method Favored by Blacks," MSNBC, February 25, 2014.
Kevin Schaul	"How Ranked-Choice Voting Works," *Star Tribune* (Minneapolis, MN), November 6, 2013.
Jim Siegel	"ACLU Sues to Reverse Ohio's Early-Voting Changes," *Columbus Dispatch* (Ohio), May 2, 2014.
Scott Wilson	"Bipartisan Election Commission Releases List of Suggested Fixes," *Washington Post*, January 22, 2014.
Jeff Zdrale	"New Early Voting Law Not About Fairness at All," *Post-Crescent* (Appleton, WI), May 8, 2014.

For Further Discussion

Chapter 1

1. In his opinion in *Shelby County v. Holder*, Chief Justice John Roberts says that "history did not end in 1965." What do you think he means by this statement, and how does it apply to the decision passed down by the justices in their ruling regarding Section 4 of the Voting Rights Act?

2. Ari Berman argues that the Voting Rights Amendment Act introduced in Congress strengthens voting rights protections and gives the federal government new ways to fight voting discrimination. Hans A. von Spakovsky, on the other hand, argues that the legislation will make race a primary factor in the election process. With which author do you agree, and why?

3. In her opinion, Sandhya Bathija argues that Section 5 of the Voting Rights Act enhances democracy by protecting minorities' right to vote. Do you think that Bathija makes a strong argument? Why, or why not?

Chapter 2

1. Richard L. Hasen points out that after the decision in *Shelby County v. Holder* North Carolina passed a bill that would, among other things, cut a week off early voting, which in previous elections was used by up to 70 percent of African American voters. In your opinion, did North Carolina pass these voting laws to restrict minorities' ability to vote, or were these changes to voting procedure needed to protect the integrity of voting and prevent voter fraud as argued by Mark H. Creech in his viewpoint? Explain.

2. Garrett Epps points out that the Constitution requires a "standard of scrutiny" in voting rights cases. What does Epps mean by this, and how does he relate that to Pennsylvania's proposed voter ID law?

Chapter 3

1. Jim Kouri argues that illegal immigrants are voting fraudulently in American elections and are violating Americans' rights. How might noncitizens' voting infringe on Americans' rights? Explain.

2. Amy Bingham points out that voter fraud is not a serious problem, because there is little motivation for an individual to impersonate someone else to cast a vote that could lead to prison, a fine, or even deportation. In light of this, do you think voter ID laws are necessary? Explain.

3. Candice Bernd explains that some states permanently disenfranchise individuals who have some kind of criminal conviction. Do you think convicted criminals should have the right to vote? Explain.

Chapter 4

1. Philip Bump argues that elections are about politics; therefore, voting reform cannot be bipartisan. Michael Waldman, on the other hand, argues that bipartisan election reforms can make voting more equitable. With which author do you agree, and why?

2. Adam Serwer argues that bilingual ballots protect voting rights and that doing away with them would disenfranchise millions of voters. In contrast, Linda Chavez argues that bilingual ballots make it easier for noncitizens to vote illegally. In your opinion, are bilingual ballots needed in the United States? Why, or why not?

3. Lawrence R. Jacobs and Joanne M. Miller and David Schultz discuss Minneapolis's process of ranked-choice

voting, a system in which voters rank up to three preferred candidates, and the candidates with the least
amount of votes are eliminated until one receives the majority of votes. Do you think ranked-choice voting should
exist on a national level? Why, or why not?

Organizations to Contact

The editors have compiled the following list of organizations concerned with the issues debated in this book. The descriptions are derived from materials provided by the organizations. All have publications or information available for interested readers. The list was compiled on the date of publication of the present volume; the information provided here may change. Be aware that many organizations take several weeks or longer to respond to inquiries, so allow as much time as possible.

American Civil Liberties Union (ACLU)
125 Broad Street, 18th Floor, New York, NY   10004
(212) 549-2500
website: www.aclu.org/voting-rights

The American Civil Liberties Union (ACLU) strives to protect and expand the freedom of all Americans to cast a ballot that will count. Through litigation, legislation, and voter education, the ACLU works to ensure that all eligible voters have an opportunity to vote, makes voting as easy and accessible as possible, and makes sure that all votes are counted equally. The ACLU further works to fight statewide voter suppression, promote electoral reforms to increase access to registration, and eradicate racial discrimination in voting. The ACLU website offers videos, case studies, articles, reports, and blog posts such as "Putting the Brakes on Voter Suppression in North Carolina" and "For Early Voting, One Size Doesn't Fit All."

American National Election Studies
Center for Political Studies, PO Box 1248
Ann Arbor, MI   48106-1248
(734) 764-5494 • fax: (734) 764-3341
e-mail: anes@electionstudies.org
website: www.electionstudies.org

American National Election Studies (ANES) is a collaboration of the University of Michigan and Stanford University that is also supported by the National Science Foundation. ANES's objective is to educate the American public about voting rights and election matters. ANES analyzes voting patterns and election issues in the United States and prepares reports and studies for government officials, the media, and the general population.

Brennan Center for Justice

161 Avenue of the Americas, 12th Floor, New York, NY 10013
e-mail: brennancenter@nyu.edu
website: www.brennancenter.org/issues/voting-rights-elections

The Brennan Center for Justice at New York University School of Law advocates for voting rights for all Americans. Through policy papers, litigation, advocacy, and education, the center works to ensure that voting is fair and accessible for all eligible citizens. The center advocates for the enfranchisement of persons with past criminal convictions, works to modernize the voter registration system, and aims to help young voters understand the different state laws and rules about how to register and vote. The center's reports include "The Case for Voter Registration Modernization" and "The Truth About Voter Fraud."

Cato Institute

1000 Massachusetts Avenue NW, Washington, DC 20001
(202) 842-0200 • fax: (202) 842-3490
website: www.cato.org

The Cato Institute is a nonprofit research center that advances limited government and individual responsibility. The institute has produced several studies and research projects on voting rights. The organization publishes reports, policy studies, and periodicals, including the *Cato Journal*, the *Cato Policy Report*, and the quarterly *Regulation* magazine. Articles such as "The Voting Rights Act Doesn't Reflect Current Political Conditions" and "The Voting Rights Act Is Outmoded, Unworkable" can be found on the Cato website.

Center for Equal Opportunity (CEO)
7700 Leesburg Pike, Suite 231, Falls Church, VA   22043
(703) 442-0066 • fax: (703) 442-0449
website: www.ceousa.org

The Center for Equal Opportunity (CEO) opposes the expansion of voting rights to immigrants until they achieve citizenship. CEO also takes an active stance in regard to the voting rights of rehabilitated felons, proposing the right to vote be reinstated after the felon fulfills his sentence and goes through a review process. Articles such as "Felon Voting," "The Voting Rights Act Goes to the Supreme Court," and "Voting Rights and Wrongs," by the organization's president and general counsel Roger Clegg, can be found on the CEO website.

Center for Information and Research on Civic Learning and Engagement (CIRCLE)
Jonathan M. Tisch College of Citizenship and Public Service
Lincoln Filene Hall, Tufts University, Medford, MA   02155
e-mail: surbhi.godsay@tufts.edu
website: www.civicyouth.org

The Center for Information and Research on Civic Learning and Engagement (CIRCLE) conducts research of youth voting and civic engagement of those between the ages of fifteen and twenty-five. CIRCLE provides information on youth voting, which is available on its website, and oversees projects to promote civic-mindedness among young people. CIRCLE recently launched an innovative, interactive map on its website that provides historical, state-by-state data on young people's electoral engagement in the past thirty years of midterm and presidential elections. The website also provides past issues of the *Around the CIRCLE* newsletter as well as a blog.

Center for Voting Technology Research
University of Connecticut, School of Engineering
261 Glenbrook Road, Unit 2237, Storrs, CT   06269-2237
(860) 486-3698
website: http://voter.engr.uconn.edu

The Center for Voting Technology Research, also known as the VoTeR Center, was created at the University of Connecticut to assist the state of Connecticut in transitioning to e-voting. The VoTeR Center subsequently undertook a range of studies and projects to test the integrity of e-voting machines and supply recommendations on the effectiveness of the voting systems. The center's website contains a series of downloadable reports on e-voting practices and machines, including descriptions of how current devices are vulnerable to hacking and fraud.

Heritage Foundation

214 Massachusetts Avenue NE, Washington, DC 20002-4999
(202) 546-4400
website: www.heritage.org

The Heritage Foundation is a conservative public policy research institute that supports the principles of free enterprise and limited government. Its many publications include the monthly *Policy Review*, position papers, fact sheets, reports, and articles. *The Foundry* blog, available on the foundation's website, features posts such as "Voting Rights: Anything but Non-Partisan" and "Supreme Court to Congress on Voting Rights Act: 'History Did Not End in 1965.'"

League of Women Voters

1730 M Street NW, Suite 1000, Washington, DC 20036-4508
(202) 429-1965 • fax: (202) 429-0854
website: www.lwv.org

The League of Women Voters was founded in 1920, the year women won the right to vote in the United States. The organization works to ensure that all eligible voters—particularly first-time voters, non-college youth, new citizens, minorities, the elderly, and low-income Americans—have the opportunity and the information to exercise their right to vote. Its website features press releases, speeches, testimony, news clips, and articles, including "Protecting and Engaging Voters" and "League Continues to Push to Restore the Voting Rights Act." Its website also offers the *Rights Now: Voices of the League* blog.

Migration Policy Institute (MPI)

1400 Sixteenth Street NW, Suite 300, Washington, DC   20036
(202) 266-1940
e-mail: info@migrationpolicy.org
website: www.migrationinformation.org

The Migration Policy Institute (MPI) is a nonpartisan, non-profit research organization that studies issues concerning the migration of people, including immigrant voting rights. MPI works with groups around the world to prepare studies on individual countries and to determine broad trends in immigration worldwide. MPI's website contains a variety of studies, reports, and articles, including "State Access to Federal Immigration Data Stirs New Controversy in Debate over Voting Rights" and "Immigrant Voting Rights Receive More Attention."

Project Vote

805 Fifteenth Street NW, Suite 250, Washington, DC   20005
(202) 546-4173 • fax: (202) 733-4762
website: http://projectvote.org

Project Vote was founded in 1994 as Voting for America. It is a national nonpartisan, nonprofit organization that works to engage low-income and minority individuals in the civic process of voting. It works to remove all barriers to voting for underrepresented groups including low-income individuals, minorities, immigrants, and youth. Its website features a Focus on the Issues section that includes summaries and Project Vote's initiatives on issues such as early voting, voter ID laws, and felon voting rights. Its *Voting Matters* blog features articles such as "In Voting Rights Legislation, Many Proposals but Few Solutions" and "Most Americans Strongly Support Voting Rights Act, Says Report."

Project Vote Smart

One Common Ground, Philipsburg, MT   59858
(888) 868-3762

e-mail: comments@votesmart.org
website: http://votesmart.org

Project Vote Smart is a nonprofit, nonpartisan organization that seeks to expand US voting rights as broadly as possible. The project maintains biographical information on candidates and provides comparisons of officials' voting records and platforms on various issues. Its website offers the VoteEasy interactive tool that allows voters to find the best candidate to match their stance on issues such as abortion, gun control, immigration, and health care.

Southern Coalition for Social Justice
1415 West Highway 54, Suite 101, Durham, NC 27707
(919) 323-3380 • fax: (919) 323-3942
e-mail: info@southerncoalition.org
website: www.southerncoalition.org/program-areas
/voting-rights/

Founded in 2007, the Southern Coalition for Social Justice (SCSJ) is a nonprofit organization that works to protect minority voting rights. It does this by defending the Voting Rights Act, supporting fair redistricting, and minimizing elections administration practices—such as photo ID requirements and restrictions on voter registration and early voting—that disenfranchise minorities. The coalition created the Census and Redistricting Institute to provide research to communities on the redistricting process to ensure fair representation for all voters. Its blog features articles such as "Let My People Vote—the Battle to End FL Felon Disenfranchisement" and "SCSJ, ACLU Ask Federal Court to Put NC Voter Suppression Law on Hold."

Bibliography of Books

Charles S. Bullock III · *Redistricting: The Most Political Activity in America.* Lanham, MD: Rowman & Littlefield, 2010.

Charles S. Bullock III and Ronald Keith Gaddie · *The Triumph of Voting Rights in the South.* Norman: University of Oklahoma Press, 2009.

Russell Freedman · *Because They Marched: The People's Campaign for Voting Rights That Changed America.* New York: Holiday House, 2014.

John Fund · *Stealing Elections: How Voter Fraud Threatens Our Democracy.* New York: Encounter Books, 2008.

John Fund and Hans von Spakovsky · *Who's Counting?: How Fraudsters and Bureaucrats Put Your Vote at Risk.* New York: Encounter Books, 2012.

Maria Gitin · *This Bright Light of Ours: Stories from the Voting Rights Fight.* Tuscaloosa: University of Alabama Press, 2014.

Michael J. Hanmer · *Discount Voting: Voter Registration Reforms and Their Effects.* New York: Cambridge University Press, 2012.

Richard L. Hasen · *The Voting Wars: From Florida 2000 to the Next Election Meltdown.* New Haven, CT: Yale University Press, 2012.

Alexander Keyssar — *The Right to Vote: The Contested History of Democracy in the United States.* New York: Basic Books, 2009.

Roger Kimball — *The New Leviathan: The State Versus the Individual in the 21st Century.* New York: Encounter Books, 2012.

Tyson D. King-Meadows — *When the Letter Betrays the Spirit: Voting Rights Enforcement and African American Participation from Lyndon Johnson to Barack Obama.* Lanham, MD: Lexington Books, 2011.

Garrine P. Laney — *The Voting Rights Act of 1965: Historical Background and Current Issues.* Hauppauge, NY: Nova Science Publishers, 2013.

Claudio López-Guerra — *Democracy and Disenfranchisement: The Morality of Electoral Exclusions.* New York: Oxford University Press, 2014.

Gary May — *Bending Toward Justice: The Voting Rights Act and the Transformation of American Democracy.* New York: Basic Books, 2013.

Daniel McCool — *The Most Fundamental Right: Contrasting Perspectives on the Voting Rights Act.* Bloomington: Indiana University Press, 2012.

Laughlin McDonald — *American Indians and the Fight for Equal Voting Rights.* Norman: University of Oklahoma Press, 2011.

Lorraine C.
Minnite
The Myth of Voter Fraud. Ithaca, NY:
Cornell University Press, 2010.

Tamra Orr
A History of Voting Rights in America.
Hockessin, DE: Mitchell Lane
Publishers, 2012.

Spencer Overton
*Stealing Democracy: The New Politics
of Voter Suppression.* New York: W.W.
Norton, 2013.

Frances Fox
Piven, Lorraine C.
Minnite, and
Margaret Groarke
*Keeping Down the Black Vote: Race
and the Demobilization of American
Voters.* New York: New Press, 2009.

Jim Ragsdale
*Minnesota Voter ID and the National
Debate: What You Need to Know.* St.
Paul: Minnesota Historical Society,
2012.

Stanley A.
Renshon
*Noncitizen Voting and American
Democracy.* Lanham, MD: Rowman
& Littlefield, 2009.

R. Volney Riser
*Defying Disfranchisement: Black
Voting Rights Activism in the Jim
Crow South, 1890–1908.* Baton
Rouge: Louisiana State University,
2013.

Christina Rivers
*The Congressional Black Caucus,
Minority Voting Rights, and the U.S.
Supreme Court.* Ann Arbor:
University of Michigan Press, 2012.

Orlando J. Rodriguez — *Vote Thieves: Illegal Immigration, Redistricting, and Presidential Elections.* Washington, DC: Potomac Books, 2011.

Mark Rosenkranz — *White Male Privilege: A Study of Racism in America 50 Years After the Voting Rights Act.* Fourth Edition. Pleasanton, CA: Law Dog Books, 2012.

Richard K. Scher — *The Politics of Disenfranchisement: Why Is It So Hard to Vote in America?* New York: M.E. Sharpe, 2011.

David Schultz — *Election Law and Democratic Theory.* Burlington, VT: Ashgate, 2014.

Abigail Thernstrom — *Voting Rights—and Wrongs: The Elusive Quest for Racially Fair Elections.* Washington, DC: American Enterprise Institute, 2009.

Laurence Tribe and Joshua Matz — *Uncertain Justice: The Roberts Court and the Constitution.* New York: Henry Holt, 2014.

James Thomas Tucker — *The Battle over Bilingual Ballots: Language Minorities and Political Access Under the Voting Rights Act.* Burlington, VT: Ashgate Publishing, 2009.

Tova Andrea Wang — *The Politics of Voter Suppression: Defending and Expanding Americans' Right to Vote.* Ithaca, NY: Cornell University Press, 2012.

Gary Watkins   *Voting Fraud in the USA*. Seattle, WA:
                   CreateSpace, 2014.

Index

W